WHEN CULTURES
CLASH

WHEN CULTURES CLASH

CLASH

Strategies for Strengthening Police-Community Relations

SECOND EDITION

DANIEL P. CARLSON

Institute for Law Enforcement Administration

PEARSON

Prentice
Hall

Upper Saddle River, New Jersey 07458

Library of Congress Cataloging-in-Publication Data

Carlson, Daniel P.
    When cultures clash: strategies for strengthening police-community relations /
Daniel P. Carlson.—2nd ed.
        p. cm.
    Includes bibliographical references and index.
    ISBN 0-13-113797-2
    1. Police-community relations. 2. Police-community relations—United States.
3. Police—United States. I. Title.

HV7936.P8C327 2005
363.2'3—dc22   2003064681

Editor-in-Chief: Stephen Helba
Executive Editor: Frank Mortimer, Jr.
Assistant Editor: Korrine Dorsey
Marketing Manager: Tim Peyton
Editorial Assistant: Barbara Rosenberg
Managing Editor: Mary Carnis
Production Liaison: Brian Hyland
Production Editor: Janet Bolton
Director of Manufacturing and Production: Bruce Johnson
Manufacturing Manger: Ilene Sanford
Manufacturing Buyer: Cathleen Petersen
Cover Design: Amy Rosen
Cover Photo: Lisette Le Bon/SuperStock
Interior Design: Janet Bolton
Composition: Integra

Proofreader: Maine Proofreading Services
Copy Editor: Maine Proofreading Services

Pearson Prentice Hall™ is a trademark of Pearson Education, Inc.
Pearson® is a registered trademark of Pearson plc
Prentice Hall® is a registered trademark of Pearson Education, Inc.

Pearson Education LTD.
Pearson Education Australia PTY, Limited
Pearson Education Singapore, Pte. Ltd.
Pearson Education North Asia Ltd.
Pearson Education Canada, Ltd.

Pearson Educacion de Mexico, S.A. de C.V.
Pearson Education—Japan
Pearson Education Malaysia, Pte. Ltd.
Pearson Education, Upper Saddle River, New Jersey

ISBN 0-13-113797-2

In policing, the relationship with a partner is special. That person, after all, is the one to whom a cop looks for physical protection, moral support, wise counsel, and a strong shoulder to lean on. I have been blessed with the best of partners for more than thirty-seven years, and this is dedicated to her, my wife, Bonnie.

Daniel Carlson

BRIEF CONTENTS

CONTENTS

7

WHO WILL POLICE THE POLICE? 88

8

CITIZEN BEHAVIOR SKILLS 100

9

MAKING A COMPLAINT AGAINST THE POLICE 109

10

BRIDGING THE GAP BETWEEN CITIZENS AND POLICE   122

11

THE NOBILITY OF POLICING   137

INTRODUCTION

As Rodney King stepped to the microphone on May 1, 1992, much of the south-central area of Los Angeles, California, was in flames. The first trial of the four Los Angeles Police Department officers accused of beating him had resulted in a virtual full acquittal two days earlier, and many citizens were expressing their outrage over what they believed to be an unjust verdict. As the television cameras focused on King, the city seemed close to anarchy, with the police overmatched, the National Guard activated, and the Federal Bureau of Investigation (FBI) sent in with orders to bring order to chaos. As the crowd of media representatives gradually quieted, King finally spoke. In a halting voice, he said simply, "Can't we all just get along?"

When King's words went out over the airwaves, police officers nationwide scoffed, unable to believe that the man who appeared to be at the center of the turmoil engulfing Los Angeles would dare say such a thing. But King was touching on an important issue many officers were unwilling to acknowledge and asking a question that continues to resonate today. Let's face it: in the arena of police-citizen interactions, the waters are often muddy. Citizens are frequently woefully uninformed about the role and limits of law enforcement, and street cops often fail to fully appreciate the manner in which their routine (and right) behaviors affect the ways in which citizens respond.

I have spent the past fifteen years deeply involved in teaching cultural diversity and ethics courses before law enforcement groups across North America. In my view, police officers, by and large, are good people doing extremely important work under difficult and dangerous circumstances. But having to discuss things like cultural diversity and ethics does not rank high on their list of favorite things to do. Very often in the heat of these classes, officers bemoan the fact that while they are "forced" to endure training designed to improve police-citizen interactions, no such training program exists for citizens. In other words, some officers say citizens need to learn how to behave around police officers and not the other way around.

Maintaining that citizens are the root cause of difficulty in police-citizen contacts is an interesting—and entirely self-serving—argument for law enforcement practitioners to make. Obviously, this point of view ignores the fact that citizens who interact with the police are very often upset, confused, intoxicated, or enraged about some personal issue. Under these circumstances, it is the responsibility of the police officer, not the citizen, to keep the situation calm and under control. Cops who believe and behave otherwise have abdicated their authority and created a volatile environment in terms of officer safety.

On the other hand, those disgruntled officers have a point. There is genuine merit in having citizens understand as much as possible about the working world of the police officer, and many agencies are exploring ways of encouraging citizen involvement. Efforts such as citizen police academies, training in cultural diversity, and respect-driven programs such as the Courtesy, Professionalism, and Respect (CPR) initiative in New York City have begun to open many doors and create bridges of communication and understanding between the police and the communities they serve. Some of these undertakings are discussed and examined in Chapter 10. Such efforts are very different from police review boards and the discussion of civilian oversight of police, notions we look at in Chapter 7.

As a retired cop with twenty-one years of full-time law enforcement experience, I have enormous affection for police officers and respect what they do for a living. It should come as no surprise, then, that much of this work is a reflection of what I discovered—sometimes the hard way—as a cop out on the street. One valuable lesson I learned, for example, was that if I got into a physical altercation with someone, it did not make any difference whether the color of the uniform I happened to be wearing was blue, tan, or gray; if that guy punched me, it hurt. Or if I had to wrestle somebody to the pavement, skin my knees, tear my clothing, break my wristwatch, and injure my back in order to arrest him, that was uncomfortable. Armed with this knowledge, I decided there *had* to be a better way of doing some of the things I was doing. One way was taking personal responsibility for communicating effectively with the other person, for example, or ignoring some insult in favor of taking someone into custody without a fight. In short, I tried to resolve each situation so everyone, including me, walked away unhurt and maybe feeling better about things.

I recall teaching a class some years ago titled Improving Police-Citizen Contacts in which I laid that very idea on the table before the group. Sometimes, I suggested to the street officers in the room, it may be strategically wise to tolerate some verbal abuse from an upset citizen to avoid provoking a much larger confrontation. As soon as I said that, a young officer sounded off loud and clear: "Nonsense" (actually, the word he used was much more colorful, but I've cleaned it up here). "When you let someone get away with showing you disrespect," he said, "you can never regain it."

When the young man was finished, a senior officer in the back of the room raised his hand and asked to speak. When he did, he directed his remarks squarely at the young officer, saying, "It's obvious you've never had your ass kicked." The younger man looked at the speaker in shock as the older fellow continued, "You've never been dragged up and down the street by the back of your Sam Browne (utility) belt over a simple traffic ticket, have you?" In other words, he was saying, experience sometimes brings wisdom, tolerance, patience, and a clear focus on what the outcome should be for every police-citizen encounter.

Police officers who are accused of acting too quickly or aggressively in taking enforcement action often voice the popular maxim, "I'd rather be judged by twelve than carried by six." In other words, facing trial for one's actions is better than being mourned at a police funeral. The obvious flaw in this mind-set is that it assumes there are only two options: twelve or six. It ignores the wide range of choices between those two poles, including that of doing a job well, going home safe at the end of the shift, and knowing that my efforts have made a positive difference in the lives of the people in the community I serve.

In the early years of the twenty-first century, the criminal justice system faces a crisis of confidence and trust. In response, the International Association of Chiefs of Police and other professional organizations are exploring and reporting on a variety of ways to measure levels of faith in law enforcement, while the media provide regular updates on whether things are getting better or worse. But as the debate rages, street cops are clear on one absolutely irrefutable fact: When citizens lack trust in law enforcement, the job of being a police officer becomes much, much more difficult.

An article by Rovella titled "Cop Scandals Take Toll" in the *National Law Journal* (May 22, 2000) argues that trust in law enforcement has been severely damaged already; it points out that some criminal prosecutors find they now must work to convince jurors that an officer testifying in court is an honest public servant and "not a liar, thief, torturer or murderer." One member of the Los Angeles County district attorney's office says that drug busts, in which the case relies almost exclusively on the testimony of police officers, are particularly difficult. As a result, he makes it a practice to call on civilians to back up police testimony. "Unless you have a civilian witness," he says, "it's going to be a lot tougher to get the jury to convict."

In Brooklyn, New York, prosecutors openly express their concerns about declining officer credibility, linking diminished trust with cases being thrown out of court. Following the shooting of Amadou Diallo in February 1999, for example, prosecutors in that borough lost the next five homicide cases that came to verdict. And when three of the New York Police Department (NYPD) officers involved in the assault on Abner Louima were convicted of obstructing justice in March 2000, eight cases that came to verdict the next day ended in acquittal. Not surprisingly, defense attorneys across the country are flashing headlines about police scandals in front of juries saying, "Maybe one day we could have believed police officers, but look what happened in New York."

Along with the pervasive sense of mistrust some people feel, there are other sources of tension between the police and large parts of the communities they serve as well. I felt that tension during my career as a police officer. I feel it even more deeply and with considerably more clarity now that I am retired and no longer on the job. A major source of that tension is easy to identify because it links directly to the inability of many active police officers and leaders to hear, understand, and respond appropriately to a citizen who complains about a lack of courtesy, respect, or responsiveness from those who are sworn to serve and protect them; the rigidity and faceless bureaucracy of policing become fully evident only when one is on the outside looking in. Police officers often complain inaccurately that "Citizens don't like us" and use that argument as a convenient alibi for keeping the public at arm's length. This strategy only serves to further strengthen some citizens' view that the police are unfeeling and unfettered and can act with impunity since they have little fear of being taken to task for misbehavior.

Perhaps a personal example will help to make the point. In mid-1994, I had the opportunity to experience something I had successfully avoided for most of my adult life: after more than thirty years as a licensed driver, I received a traffic ticket. It was for an administrative violation (I had failed to renew the registration on my vehicle), and an alert police officer pulled me over for that offense as I was driving home from work. I fully deserved the summons that day, but the otherwise unprofessional treatment I received was wholly unwarranted. I understand the importance of good officer safety skills and appreciate the "bladed stance, hand on weapon" posture of the officer as I opened the glove compartment for my insurance card. But when it should have been evident that I was who I actually appeared to be (an otherwise upstanding citizen who had committed a minor violation of the law), there was no shift in the style or demeanor of the officer. When I asked several questions about the violation and how I should go about handling the ticket, for example, I received responses that were curt and, in one case, inaccurate. I decided to complain to the police department about the way I was treated.

Before contacting the police department, I paid the fine for the violation I had committed. I did so, of course, because I did not want anyone to think I was complaining in order to have the ticket dismissed. In my letter to the chief of police, I described my law enforcement background, including the fact that I had investigated a number of service complaints during my twenty-one years of police experience. As a result, I felt qualified to distinguish between behaviors that could be categorized as businesslike and professional and those that were simply abrupt and rude. And as I pointed out to the chief, I felt I had been treated in a thoroughly unprofessional fashion that day. I also told him that I would very much like to hear from him about this matter. I continue to await a formal written reply.

That is not to say there was no response. About a month after I sent my letter of complaint to the chief, I received a phone call one Saturday evening from a clearly unhappy sergeant who left no doubt about his displeasure at having been ordered to make contact with some whining citizen (me) and to set me straight about a few things. After several perfunctory questions about the particulars of my complaint and what I expected to have done about it, he got right to the point: "This is a dangerous town, so we have to treat everyone like they are a threat to us." And although he did not come right out and say it, he left no doubt that his view on handling complaints like mine was essentially to let me know three things: (1) we're the police, (2) you need us, and (3) shut up.

Ignoring the blatant ignorance of his remark, I pointed out that in my view he had just put his finger on the precise source of the problem. Yes, officers must be alert to officer safety issues and highly trained in street survival techniques. But they must also be able to shift gears when they find that different skills might be appropriate to a situation. And although I made sure to thank him for having called me, I was left feeling angry, frustrated, and poorly served.

Now, remember, I am describing an encounter as a retired police officer, and one who actually supports police officers and loves the police profession. Imagine how maddening such a response must be to someone who doesn't feel the same affection for law enforcement as I do. It could be argued that, as with many issues, people tend to be distributed along a bell-shaped curve, with a small number of true believers in law enforcement and the police at one end and an equally small number of antipolice individuals at the other. To people on one end, the police can do no wrong; to those on the other, the police can do no right. In the middle remain the majority of citizens, who know there is such a thing as a police department in their community but don't give it a lot of thought unless they are forced into some sort of contact with it; in other words, most people are ambivalent about law enforcement. If this is true, then one can only speculate about the way in which experiences like mine might contribute to the growing level of mistrust and dissatisfaction that police departments so often complain about.

Few people would disagree with the notion that police officers perform a valuable service in the community. However, there are extraordinary differences between the way many citizens and cops view the job of law enforcement. To illustrate this point, Chapter 1 looks at those things citizens have a legitimate right to expect from the police in their communities. In contrast, Chapter 2 outlines a range of differences between the citizen view and the police view of what law enforcement is really all about. As a separate matter, the police culture has a powerful effect on the way police officers see themselves, their peers, and the larger community they are sworn to serve. Chapter 3 therefore examines some of the very unique constraints and duties that this close-knit society imposes on its members.

The issue of officer safety is addressed in Chapter 4, which outlines for citizens, in particular, some of the reasons police officers behave the way they do in their dealings with the public. In Chapter 5 we look at the ways in which the noble mission of policing sometimes goes awry and examine a few unfortunate high-profile events of recent years, including the Amadou Diallo shooting, racial profiling, and the Rampart scandal. The wholesale failure of law enforcement management is one of the most significant (and most often ignored) reasons for the failure of the police "mission"; it is discussed at length in Chapter 6.

Chapter 7 examines the fundamental question of whether a police agency is ever capable of effectively investigating itself and explores the idea of civilian-police review. In Chapter 8, we provide information on recommended citizen behavior skills to use when interacting with the police in any official capacity. And should the need arise for a complaint to be made about police behavior (or misbehavior), Chapter 9 suggests a variety of avenues for doing so, along with an overview of information that will be needed and how it can be collected.

Chapter 10 includes a great deal of good news. Many forward-looking and thoughtful law enforcement leaders are working to improve the way their departments interact with and serve their communities, and a number of their efforts are presented and outlined here. Chapter 11, finally, is a reminder of the absolute good that most law enforcement practitioners do every day as they go about their sworn duties. There are blemishes, of course, but there is also hope.

This book, then, is for anyone interested in the state of relations between the police and the community, but especially for citizens who don't fully understand the complexity of police work and what being a cop is all about. It outlines some of the difficulties faced by those who are sworn to serve and protect while underscoring the legitimate expectation that citizens' rights be safeguarded at all times and in all circumstances. That is at the very core of a democracy. In addition, this is a how-to book for citizens; it provides strategies for avoiding conflicts that sometimes arise in face-to-face encounters with a law enforcement officer.

This book is also for police officers who, like me, have enormous faith in the law enforcement community and who, also like me, care deeply for those among us who have chosen law enforcement as their life's work. For the most part, law enforcement is populated by people who admirably do the noble, dangerous, difficult job of keeping the peace, and those thoughtful professionals will recognize themselves here. They understand and embrace the notion of police-community cooperation and interaction. Some do so because of a core belief in what their work is really all about, and some do so because of experiences in their own lives and careers. In the end, though, all agree on one central point: A police officer who treats people right and who enjoys support and understanding from the community is a safer police officer.

Not every officer is drawn to policing for the right reasons, so it is likely some not-so-thoughtful folks will see themselves here as well. In the 1970s and 1980s, the very popular and realistic television show *Hill Street Blues* gave many viewers their first peek into the seamier side of police work. Typically, each episode of this highly regarded series began with a patrol sergeant conducting a preshift lineup with his officers, a meeting he always concluded with the admonition "Be safe out there." After several years, the actor playing the part of the patrol sergeant died. The role was recast with not only a new actor but a different attitude as well. When the new patrol sergeant ended his meetings, he always gave his officers this warning: "Remember, do it to them before they do it to you."

Unfortunately, some police officers still believe the only way to do their jobs is "to kick ass first and ask questions later." Thankfully, those who believe that seem to be a disappearing breed, but they are still around. They are the few who equate restraint with weakness and a discussion of cultural understanding with an attempt to emasculate the white race. Although they are relatively few in number, other police officers know who they are and often devise elaborate strategies to avoid having to work with them. It is a good first step, but it is not enough. As Frank Serpico said in his testimony before the Knapp Commission in 1973, he longs for the day "when the bad cop will fear the good cop, and not the other way around."

For many people, a locked door is an irresistible thing. Who knows, after all, what lies on the other side? Like a number of other insular cultures, the inner world of policing keeps itself behind a locked door, and most people never have an opportunity to open that door. This book, in some small way, is intended to unlock that door and shed a bit of light on some of the darkness and mystery behind it.

A large measure of the tension that exists between police and citizens stems from a paucity of openness, communication, and unbiased information. To help correct the situation, this book attempts to provoke thought and discussion among people of good-will, regardless of their backgrounds. In the process, both the police practitioner and the average citizen will likely find the approach alternately stimulating and irritating—and that is as it should be. This book will have proved successful if, at some point, a police officer disgustedly flings it across the room, accusing me of being a traitor to the law enforcement profession. It can also be declared a success when a citizen, already upset about an encounter with law enforcement, slams it to the floor, declaring me an apologist for police. The truest indicator that this book has merit, though, will come when they both pick it up again, continue reading, and think to themselves, "You know, I never looked at it quite that way before."

The discussion to follow in these pages about the state of police-citizen cooperation and understanding is an important one. And while citizens and police alike have a stake in the way it unfolds, the September 11, 2001, terrorist attacks on the World Trade Center have, from the point of view of the criminal justice practitioner, crystallized the incredibly complex and delicate nature of this conversation. What citizen, after all, can ever again harbor a doubt about the altruism and bravery of police, fire, and rescue personnel after watching so many of them willingly climb the stairs of those doomed buildings while passing many hundreds of people descending to safety? When the heartbreaking results of that calamity became fully known, police officers were deeply touched by the torrent of support following their colleagues' selfless acts of courage. As a seemingly endless succession of funerals and memorial services took place in the fall of 2001, citizens flocked to stand beside, support, and embrace legions of grieving police officers. But painful though it may be to contemplate, it is important to ask whether that mind-set—What shall we call it?

Openness? Vulnerability? Warmth? Love?—will be permanent or transitory. We will ask that question in a variety of ways throughout this book.

To help prepare the reader, each chapter is preceded by a set of guideposts. Containing suggestions addressed separately to police officers and citizens, they provide a sort of introductory road map for the chapter that will follow, with thoughts on how and why specific issues might be of particular interest.

ACKNOWLEDGMENTS

While many individuals deserve my thanks for their support and guidance in the creation of this book, I am most of all thankful for the many wise and courageous law enforcement practitioners I have come to know and love during the course of my career. More than anyone else, these men and women have been my teachers, and I am forever grateful.

Prentice Hall would like to thank the following for reviewing the second edition of *When Cultures Clash*: Vincent Benincasa, Hesser College, Manchester, NH; Michael Grabowski, Prairie View A&M University, Prairie View, TX; Ronald Swan, Lincoln College at Normal, Normal, IL.

chapter 1

THE JOB
OF A POLICE OFFICER
(CITIZEN'S POINT OF VIEW)

To the Citizen: As you read this chapter, consider your expectations for the police in your community. As a citizen and taxpayer, how do you expect to be treated by public servants? Are there limits to what the police should do to keep the community safe? What are those limits? Beyond those discussed in the chapter, do you have other expectations for the police in your community? What are they?

To the Police Officer: As you read this chapter, consider whether there are differences in how you see your job and how citizens might see it. Is there confusion about what the public expects from you, what the department expects from you, and how you see your job? Where do those expectations conflict? After reading this chapter, which parts did you find particularly objectionable? Why?

Let's face it: We hire police officers, train them, enthuse them, and then direct them into places that most sensible human beings would never venture, telling them to protect us and keep our streets safe. We ask them to sort through and come to grips with numerous social ills that other authorities in society have long since given up on, and, most often, we ask them to do these things without letting us really see what is required to do so. And there is another very important issue. We ask the police to keep the wheels of our community turning smoothly and to make sure the less desirable members of society are kept at bay, but we want them to do it without putting any undue pressure on *us* personally.

In an interview some years ago, a former chief of the New York City Police Department was reportedly asked if it would ever be possible to clean up New York and make it safe. The chief is said to have paused for a moment and then replied, "Of course it can be done. Just give me about 100 officers and *suspend the U.S. Constitution.*" Needless to say, he was using that tongue-in-cheek suggestion to make a point: that police officers are obliged to do what they do within the constraints of the Constitution and Bill of Rights. And therein lies the rub. On the one hand, citizens (rightly) demand that the police spare no effort in making their communities safe. On the other hand, citizens (rightly) demand that the police do nothing to jeopardize their (the citizens) individual constitutional rights. Navigating that middle ground, the police often find, requires delicate and finely tuned skills.

THE ENFORCEMENT OF QUALITY OF LIFE

Although I grew up very close to New York City, I always tried to avoid spending any time there because of the enormous hassles. When I became a police officer and found myself working in areas around (but mostly outside) that huge metropolis, my opinion did not change much. Therefore, I was not particularly excited about the prospect of visiting New York for a minivacation in the spring of 1997. My youngest daughter had just completed college, so my wife and I planned to take her and her fiancé to a Broadway show and visit a number of the tourist attractions as a graduation gift. Based on my experiences, I was steeling myself for the very worst.

It had been several years since my last foray into New York, and although I had been reading about and discussing the crackdown on quality-of-life issues imposed by the mayor and police commissioner, I had not previously seen the results firsthand. That opportunity came when my companions and I took our first walk in Manhattan, and I realized the magnitude of the transition. As we walked around the clean streets, I saw no panhandlers, drunks, or apparent homeless. The taxicabs were clean, the fare for a ride was reasonable, and each cabdriver gave me a receipt instantly and without my asking. I was impressed.

Some would say I was also quite naive, because my conclusions about the positive effects of the quality-of-life crackdown had been drawn from my observations in the largely tourist areas of New York City. According to some city residents, quality-of-life enforcement has a very different meaning if you happen to reside in some of the inner-city areas less visible to casual visitors.

In New York there is a remarkable and internationally famous neighborhood known as Greenwich Village. Difficult to describe with precision, the Village is best characterized as a kind of crossroads of the world, where the rich, full mosaic of humanity comes together to celebrate through music, poetry, and so on. Many people (some who happen to live in the Village, for example) describe it in far less glowing terms. In fact, in the late 1990s, a group of Greenwich Village residents cried out for relief from New York City, complaining that they'd "had it up to here" with the behavior of that "mosaic of humanity." In particular, they said they wanted something done about the raucous bars with music blaring until all hours of the night, the street minstrels, the drug dealers, and the drunk drivers racing up and down the streets.

Hearing the call for assistance from the unhappy citizens living in Greenwich Village, the New York City Police Department responded in force, creating a quality-of-life enforcement effort known as Operation Civil Village. And it didn't take long for the effects of their work to be felt: The bars turned down the volume of their music, the drug dealers disappeared, the street minstrels left, and drunk driving no longer seemed to be a problem. Very quickly, the formerly aggrieved residents flooded the newspapers with laudatory letters to the editor, complimenting the police for a job well done.

Within a year, though, the tone of those letters to the editor began to change. Law enforcement efforts that had previously met with boundless praise suddenly seemed open to question. Citizens who had only recently backed the police so strenuously now wrote letters conveying the following sentiments: "Yes, the police did a good job. But *I live here.* And *I'm* getting tired of having to produce identification for a cop every hundred yards when *I'm* simply out for a walk in the evening. And, furthermore, *I* don't think *I* should have to go through three drunk-driving road checks every time *I* drive down *my* street."

In effect, these residents of Greenwich Village were saying that heavy-duty enforcement of quality-of-life violations is acceptable as long as *those people* are the ones feeling the heat of aggressive police action. However, when *we* begin to feel the pinch of some of those same efforts we countenance for others . . . when *our* freedom of movement becomes limited . . . when *we* find *our* belongings searched repeatedly and without justification . . . when *we* are asked to present an ID to a police officer simply for walking down the street, only then do we seem prepared to speak up. In this case it happened to be the residents of Greenwich Village rising up in protest, but their position is shared by a great many other citizens.

In a democracy, the police derive their power and authority from the citizens they police. And when they go about doing the job of law enforcement, they do it with citizens' consent. Consequently, as they do what we have hired them to do, each of us has a legitimate right to expect close adherence to certain principles of professional law enforcement. These five principles—balanced enforcement of the law, openness and accessibility, accountability, police officer adherence to the oath of office, and objective enforcement of the law—are described in the following sections.

Balanced Enforcement of the Law

The issue of balanced enforcement speaks directly to the quandary of citizens in Greenwich Village. It is a fundamental question about the degree of government intrusion we are willing to endure in our everyday lives, and it asks us to consider what price we are willing to pay for an absolutely safe community. For example, most of us would agree that eliminating the sale and use of illegal drugs from our communities is a good thing. If so, we have to carefully consider what we are willing to put up with as law-abiding citizens in order to achieve that end. Random warrantless searches of our homes? Confining suspects incommunicado during investigations? Death penalty for convicted drug dealers?

For the police, the issue of balanced enforcement touches a deep chord when it comes to things such as high-speed pursuits. Many cops believe fervently that it is important to pursue any and all violators and that a failure to do so symbolizes blatant disrespect for the law. Many citizens and police administrators, incidentally, agree—up to a point. It is important to capture wrongdoers, especially those who have committed serious crimes, but at what cost? From 1995 to 1999, ninety-seven people died in the state of Georgia as a result of police chases. Read that number again: *ninety-seven* people (a figure which includes people being chased, innocent bystanders, and police officers). From the standpoint of balanced enforcement, then, there are two important questions: (1) What level of highway carnage are we willing to accept in order that every violator be aggressively pursued? and (2) How much financial liability should citizens be asked to endure in accounting for such losses?

In terms of balanced enforcement, citizens also have a right to expect officers to be sensitive to both the spirit of the law and the letter of the law. When a cop stops a fifteen-year-old station wagon with a faulty muffler on Christmas Eve, with a down-on-their-luck mom and dad in the front seat and five kids in the back, the officer doesn't *have to* write the driver a ticket (even though he could). When two neighbors who just finished cutting their lawns on a hot summer day are sitting on their riding mowers on the shoulder of the road where their yards adjoin, talking and drinking a beer, the officer who spots them doesn't *have to* arrest them for an open container violation (even though she could). An actual quality-of-life enforcement action from New York City (see box on pages 6–7) makes the point perfectly.

Openness and Accessibility

If citizens have a complaint or concern about any aspect of law enforcement, there should be an open and agreeable means by which their comments can be heard and responded to. Look at it this way: Every reputable company providing a product or service to the public has an expectation (a hope, really) that unhappy customers will give it feedback on why they were dissatisfied. This is crucial information a company needs to make its product or service better. As "consumers" of law enforcement services, then, should citizens be willing to accept anything less?

Many law enforcement leaders have worked hard to make their agencies more accessible and open (see Chapter 10), but much remains to be done in this regard. At the end of the day, though, police departments are *public-sector* organizations, and law enforcement officers are *public servants*. It is important to remember who works for whom.

The issue of openness and accessibility also speaks to the manner in which departments provide their services across their entire community. The style of policing deemed acceptable in one

LIFE SUFFERS IN THE NAME OF QUALITY

Decide for yourself whether enforcement of the law was fair in the following case and, if so, whether fair also means sensible. The tale is offered without judgement. Sort of.

Its main characters are a married couple, Rachel Thompson and Rev. Joseph Gilmore. He is senior minister at the South Presbyterian Church in Dobbs Ferry, N.Y. She just finished her second year at Union Theological Seminary in Morningside Heights. Hell-raising youngsters they are not.

Last Friday, after her final exam, on medieval church history, Ms. Thompson went to her car. A rose was pinned under a windshield wiper.

"I looked around for my husband," she said. (How many women can take for granted that their husbands are behind an unexpected romantic gesture?) Sure enough, there was Gilmore, carrying champagne on ice, two fluted glasses and hand-woven napkins—a surprise to celebrate the end of classes.

Off they went to tiny Sakura Park, by Grant's Tomb. They sat sipping their champagne on a glorious late afternoon, while the bells of Riverside Church pealed and the light, in Gilmore's words, "drifted down like gold dust."

Does it get any better? "You know how bliss can catch you sideways?" Ms. Thompson said. "This was one of those times when bliss came up straight away."

And then came three police officers.

In near-silence, they handed the couple two summonses each, written up as "open alcohol in public" and "possessing alcohol in park to consume." Ms. Thompson and Gilmore must go next month to Criminal Court, where they each face possible fines of up to $250.

So much for bliss.

As one officer recorded the violations, Ms. Thompson said, she and her husband tried to explain themselves, first by noting their religious roles. It was, she acknowledged later, a pretty lame point. "I realize I am skating on very thin ice," she said.

Certainly, the ticket-writing officer was unimpressed. "Quality of life," she said in a low growl, according to the couple. She handed them the summonses and walked off with her colleagues.

"It was weird," Ms. Thompson said. "It just wasn't a human interaction. If only they'd asked why we were drinking. He could have been proposing marriage for all they knew, me with a rose in my lap."

O.K., what do we have here? Nondiscriminatory law enforcement, an admirable notion? Or mindless application of City Hall's vaunted "zero tolerance" for any stain on the civic fabric?

On one hand, the couple were far from making public nuisances of themselves; they were the picture of romance, some would say. Couldn't the police have simply warned them to put the bottle away without any harm being done to the Republic?

On the other hand, who gets to decide that a middle-aged suburban couple's drinking Korbel in the park is a loftier pursuit than two street types' passing their white lightning back and forth?

Then again, the police make such distinctions all the time. Tolerance is never at absolute zero. The beer flows freely and publicly at family picnics held on warm-weather weekends in northern reaches of Riverside Park. So does the pinot grigio at summertime concerts in Central Park. You don't see summonses when Mozart is in the air.

"We tell officers to use their discretion," said Edward T. Norris, the Deputy Police Commissioner for operations. Still, he said, the law against public consumption of alcohol "is something we want to enforce—it has been a successful cornerstone of our quality of life campaign." There certainly has been no shortage of summonses: 26,841 in the first four months of this year, by far the most for any "quality of life" offense.

Another point, said Edward Skyler, a Parks Department spokesman, is that "it's not up to any one person to decide" when it is all right to flout the ban on public drinking.

Gilmore says he is well aware of that. But he argues that the officers in Sakura Park were "seeing the law with one eye."

"There's no depth perception with one eye," he said. "You see the facts but not the context." If anything, he asserted, this sweet, innocent interlude on a sun-dappled day enhanced the quality of city life.

Many might agree. All the same, "we'll plead guilty," Ms. Thompson said. "And throw ourselves on the mercy of a champagne-loving judge," she added.

neighborhood should be similar to the style used in another neighborhood across town. For instance, in a span of only a couple of months in the spring of 1999, New York City Police Department "entry teams" went into wrong apartments on six different occasions in the execution of search warrants. In one case, they broke down a door at 6:15 A.M., rolled in a stun grenade, and "captured" a retired baker, his middle-aged wife, and their eighteen-year-old developmentally disabled daughter who was taking a shower at the time. When they realized their error, the official reaction was essentially "This is a war on drugs, and in any war there are going to be some casualties." But as a number of observers have pointed out, if the police crashed through doors in Beverly Hills, Scarsdale, or Greenwich the way they did in inner-city neighborhoods populated by people of color, you can bet the practice would be stopped in a New York minute.

Accountability

In the summer of 2000, people driving Ford Explorers with certain types of Firestone tires had very worried looks in their eyes. Seemingly out of nowhere that summer there erupted deep and widespread concerns about vehicle safety, along with the associated questions of who knew about the problems and when they first learned of them. Ford blamed Firestone, Firestone threw hard questions back at Ford, and everybody demanded to know why the National Highway Traffic Safety Administration didn't take action more quickly. As customers defected in droves, stocks plummeted, and criminal and civil investigations loomed, the CEOs of each of the companies under fire did something very important: They stood up publicly and apologized for the problem, promising they personally would spare no effort to find and correct the source of problems as quickly as possible.

Many businesses have survived a crisis through the simple act of admitting a problem and outlining what is being done to improve things. Unfortunately, this philosophy is sometimes lost on law enforcement leaders. In September 2000, for example, a Prince Georges County, Maryland, undercover police officer followed a car into northern Virginia, where he became involved in a confrontation with the driver of the car he was trailing. The officer shot and killed the other man. The use of deadly force in this case may turn out to be entirely justified, but it was hard to say at the time because, despite cries for information from citizens and the media, the chief of police remained silent for four days before making any public comment. It is noteworthy that the chief chose to stand mute despite the fact that in the preceding thirteen months his police officers had shot twelve people, killing five of them.

Some departments, on the other hand, seem to deal appropriately with crisis situations. For example, in the late 1990s, in Boston, a drug raid in a housing project went badly awry one afternoon. A warrant execution team received faulty information about the address they were supposed to enter, and when they broke down the door and charged into the wrong apartment, an elderly citizen (a seventy-eight-year-old retired minister) in the home suffered a heart attack and died. Members of the police department immediately did something that shocked many observers: They stood up publicly and announced they had made a mistake.

The Boston police commissioner went to the wake and funeral for the deceased citizen, and in an effort to ensure (as much as possible) that such a terrible thing did not happen again, he ordered a very public investigation into the circumstances of the errant drug raid. Needless to say, community residents were unhappy that an innocent life had been lost as a result of police action, but the police department's forthright approach and willingness to be accountable for its mistake ameliorated the outrage that often accompanies this type of situation.

Police Officer Adherence to the Oath of Office

Every sworn officer starts a law enforcement career in exactly the same way, by taking an oath of office. And although the exact words may vary slightly from one jurisdiction to the next, there is usually common reference to such things as honor, duty, and an obligation to support and defend the Constitution of the United States. But an oath is really much more than the collection of words uttered at a swearing-in ceremony. At its core, an oath is a contract . . . a deal . . . a promise officers make to their community about what they will do while in its employ and how they will do it. And when a promise is made, other people have a legitimate right to expect that it will be kept.

We citizens have given the police tremendous power in our communities, but we have done so with the expectation that it will be used fairly, openly, and equitably. We place enormous trust in those we hire to keep us safe and protect our rights. Knowing, for example, that police officers could, if they chose to, strip a citizen of his or her constitutional liberties at whim, we trust they will use their powers of arrest appropriately. When we give police officers the authority to take a human life under certain circumstances, we trust they will remain ever mindful of the gravity and potential consequences of that awesome power.

The issue of trust permeates every aspect of the relationship between citizens and police but is seldom more evident than in a court of law. The viability of the entire criminal justice system can be said to rest on faith in the simple word of a police officer who has sworn to tell the truth, the whole truth, and nothing but the truth. For us citizens, this means that when officers complete their testimony under oath, our response should be a simple "Okay." In other words, there should not be a scintilla of doubt that what the officers said was absolutely truthful.

Most police officers understand that taking an oath has special weight and meaning and that citizens have elevated expectations of them as a result. In classroom discussions, officers acknowledge that citizens have a right to hold them to a higher standard of conduct than others in society, pointing to the oath as one justification for that belief. Anyone who doubts the existence of a higher standard for police who violate the law need only review the court transcripts when sentences are handed down to corrupt cops who have violated their oaths. In July 2000, a U.S. district judge sentenced a former police chief in Louisiana to a prison term for selling drugs. Not satisfied that the jail time adequately expressed his revulsion at the former law enforcement officer's betrayal of the public trust, the judge concluded by describing him as a "scumbag . . . dumb . . . and pathetic."

Objective Enforcement of the Law

When police officers take action in an official capacity, there is an expectation that they do so without any hint of bias or personal opinion. Most citizens (and cops) would agree with this notion, of course, but practice does not always meet the ideals of theory. Each of us carries a great deal of personal baggage accumulated over the years, and although we would like to think we are able to leave deeply held personal views out of the equation when we make decisions, it is extraordinarily difficult to do so.

Fortunately, most members of the law enforcement community understand the importance of objectivity and set their own opinions aside in the course of their official duties. At least they try to do so. Most of the time.

When it comes to highly emotional matters such as abortion, the two sides are clearly separated in our society. Many citizens hold deeply personal views on this powerful issue, so it would be foolish to think that police officers (who are citizens, too) might not identify strongly with one side or the other. But when it comes to officers being required to act in an official capacity—removing protesters from in front of an abortion clinic, for example—we expect that they will do so regardless of their personal views on the issue. And most times this is what happens.

Sometimes, though, the issue becomes even more complicated than usual. In the midst of a series of antiabortion protests in Nueces County, Texas, in the mid-1990s, the Catholic bishop in that jurisdiction made an announcement that created considerable difficulty for many cops. He said that Catholic police officers who participated in removing abortion protesters would, from his point of view, be participants in committing an abortion. For some, it was a weighty point to consider.

When it comes to emotionally charged issues such as abortion, many agencies now try to confront potential conflicts head-on. When there are planned demonstrations that will likely result in arrests, officers are often asked about moral conflicts in advance and, if necessary, given the opportunity to work in assignments that keep them away from the protests.

However, not everyone agrees with the view that officers should receive a "pass" because of some personal moral concern. Some leaders argue that once cops have the right to select the police activities they want to be excluded from, the next step will be choices on which laws they would like to enforce, followed by certain bedlam. In other words, they say, police officers acting in an official capacity must keep their personal views to themselves at all times.

The waters here get very muddy; on the one hand, there is an absolute expectation that police officers will perform their jobs objectively (meaning they set their personal views aside) and in unquestioning fashion (meaning they will follow the orders of their bosses). On the other hand, there is room for discussion about the types of people we want to seek out, recruit, and hire to be police officers in our communities in the first place. Are police departments looking for robots who will do the job without ever stopping to ask "why"? Or might law enforcement benefit from bringing in people who will do the job but who will also be willing to ask some hard questions along the way?

In his book *Character and Cops*, Edwin J. Delattre (1994) speaks to the issue of citizen expectations of police behavior in this way:

> When a person voluntarily accepts a position of public trust, he takes on new obligations. If he does not want to live up to them, he is free to decline the job. Not only is this a fair demand, but granting authority without expecting public servants to live up to it would be unfair to everyone they are expected to serve. (p. 187)

Police officers do difficult, dangerous work, and we, as citizens, should be enormously grateful for all they do on our behalf. But at the end of the day, it is important to remember that cops are *public servants*, and citizens have an absolute right to expect to be treated fairly and respectfully in every interaction, regardless of the circumstances. As Delattre points out, police officers are not drafted into the service of law enforcement; they are there by choice. If officers feel the bar of acceptable behavior is set too high, or the obligations they are expected to meet are too difficult, they all have a choice: They can (and should) leave.

DISCUSSION QUESTIONS

1. In the interest of remaining as safe and secure as possible, which of your civil liberties would you be willing to forfeit? What about due process rights for people arrested for serious offenses or suspected of being involved in terrorist activity? How far should we go in protecting that person's civil liberties?

2. Discretion is an important tool for police officers to have at their disposal. What factors should guide the use of discretion when it comes to enforcement of certain laws? In the Sakura Park vignette, should the divinity school student have been treated any differently than a homeless person drinking wine in the same vicinity? Why or why not?

3. To what degree should police officers feel bound by their oath of office? Since there are no legal sanctions requiring obedience to an oath, why should police officers feel obliged to abide by it?

4. Is it reasonable to expect a police officer to be completely objective when it comes to enforcement of the law? What bearing might the core beliefs of a police officer have on her ability to enforce a law she disagrees with? What should she do if she finds her beliefs in conflict with a law? What options are available to her agency if she is unable to enforce a law she opposes?

chapter *2*

The Job
of a Police Officer
(Police Officer's Point
of View)

To the Citizen: As you read this chapter, ask yourself whether any of the issues discussed could have a legitimate bearing on how the police do (and feel about) their jobs. Do police officers have reason to feel misunderstood and unappreciated? What do you think about the suggestion that some police officers engage in "testilying"? Can you imagine any circumstances in which you would tolerate lying by a police officer?

To the Police Officer: Before you read this chapter, consider the limits placed on you by your police department, the citizens in your community, the Bill of Rights, and even other officers. Would your job be easier and your efforts more effective if there were fewer controls on you? Which limits would you do away with in order to make you better able to do the good work of policing? Once you have perused this chapter, consider which parts you agreed with and which you disagreed with. Why?

Maybe you've been thinking about becoming a police officer. If so, be prepared to take written exams, undergo physical and psychological screening, and qualify on physical-agility tests—all before you are even eligible for hire.

    To save you a great deal of time and energy, the following list will provide insight into some of the other, less-well-known things you should know about what it takes to be a good cop. For example, you might make a good police officer if

- You believe that 25 percent of people are a waste of protoplasm.
- You call for a criminal check of anyone who seems friendly to you.
- Discussing dismemberment over a gourmet meal seems perfectly normal to you.
- You can identify a negative teeth-to-tattoo ratio just by looking at a person.
- You find humor in other people's stupidity.
- You disbelieve 90 percent of what you hear and 75 percent of what you see.
- You believe that "too stupid to live" should be a valid verdict.
- You find out a lot about paranoia just by following people around.
- At a social gathering, you are the only person introduced by profession.
- People shout "I didn't do it!" when you walk into a room, and they think it's original and hugely funny.

The foregoing list (which has circulated around policing in various forms for years and is, of course, written tongue in cheek) is intended to parody the cynicism that creeps into a police persona over time. But it provides something else as well. For the uninitiated, it is a peek at one of the most important survival tools available to a police officer: a highly developed sense of humor. Also known as "gallows humor," it allows effective cops to deal with some of the most horrific events imaginable and then later relieve tension and pain through—believe it or not—laughter.

THE ROLE OF LAW ENFORCEMENT HUMOR

Frankly, some of the things police officers are able to laugh at would repulse most citizens. One example is the story about a police officer who was sent to check on the well-being of an old woman who had not been in contact with relatives for a lengthy period. When the officer arrived at the house, he noticed more than a week's worth of newspapers piled up on the porch and flies thick on the inside of the woman's windows. Making a quick assessment of the situation, the officer turned to his partner and said, "Well, it doesn't look like the cat needs to be fed."

It is important to point out that for most police officers, the laughter associated with gallows humor is not derisive or disrespectful. Instead, it is a conscious gesture toward balance. In this form, laughter is part of the cleansing process that allows them to partition off pain and to prepare for the next victim or event. To paraphrase Mark Twain, "The human race has only one really effective weapon and that's laughter. The moment it arises, all our hardnesses yield, all our resentments slip away." Twain also said, "The basis of all humor is tragedy."

Police humor also extends to the manner in which officers laugh at each other. Cops are absolutely merciless in poking fun at one another, so much so that a citizen who overhears a conversation may wonder whether the officers really like each other. And it doesn't take long for new police officers to learn the importance of keeping their mouths shut about something they may be especially sensitive about; once the issue becomes known, every officer on the shift will go to extraordinary lengths to make sport of it. An officer with a known affection for picking up and caring for injured birds will quickly become known as "bird man," for example, and other officers will likely use his locker as a repository for any winged creatures they find dead along the shoulder of the road.

In law enforcement, one of the ways an organizational culture is passed on from generation to generation is through the telling of "war stories." As evidence, go into any squad room with cops sitting around talking before roll call and you will hear tales about officers who left years ago but whose reputations remain. And these war stories, rather than describing remarkable arrests or lifesaving actions, usually recount in vivid detail the mistakes some long-departed cop made. Like the time old so-and-so climbed into the back seat of his patrol car to catch some shut-eye on the midnight tour, forgetting that the department had just—for the first time—installed screens between the front and back seats and disabled the inside rear door handles. He sat trapped in the back of his unit for three hours until another cop found him and let him out.

Laughter and camaraderie are important elements in the world of law enforcement because they are part of the mucilage that binds police officers together. But there is a profound contradiction. On the one hand, cops tend to withdraw into their closed, tight-knit world and, at least figuratively, tell citizens to stay away. On the other hand, they want citizens to understand, support, and appreciate them for what they do.

THE COMPLEXITY OF STREET POLICING

Sometimes police officers feel terribly unappreciated. They go out every day, do good things in the community, and fight crime and/or evil, and it sometimes seems that all they ever hear is criticism. Whether it's the department command staff, the mayor, internal affairs, the American Civil Liberties Union (ACLU), or individual citizens, somebody always has a complaint about something. Officers often believe that if only these people would shut up, stay out of the way, and let the police do what needs to be done, things would be a whole lot better for everybody.

Take the situation in New Westminster, British Columbia, for example. In late 1998, the leaders of this small Canadian city about 20 kilometers from Vancouver found themselves confronting an enormous problem. The downtown business district had been overrun by crack dealers who were brazenly plying their trade on the center-city sidewalks and scaring off customers from the family restaurants and other establishments. The city leaders wanted something done and they wanted it done quickly, so they gave the police department about $200,000 in overtime money and told them to make the problem go away.

The New Westminster police accomplished the task they were assigned; in short order, the crack dealers had disappeared. In the midst of the celebration, though, a number of observers have voiced concern about the methods used to bring about what everyone would agree is a good end. CBC, a Canadian television station in Vancouver, captured many of the police tactics and strategies in a series of programs on the New Westminster efforts, and a viewing of its videotapes leaves a number of questions unanswered.

As part of their cleanup effort, for example, New Westminster officers placed unarrested young men in a police van and then drove them out to remote parts of the community, where they dropped them off one by one to find their way home. In a democracy, how can the police justify this approach? The videotape showed the police ordering an unarrested man to take $20 out of his wallet and give it to a taxi driver to take him as far out of town as that money would permit. Effective though it may be, what right do the police have to take such action? Lacking the necessary warrant to search the homes of suspected crack dealers on their own, the police brought along inspectors from the fire, health, and code enforcement departments—all groups with extensive authority to enter such premises without a warrant—in order to do so. It was an innovative way to enter someone's home, no doubt, but what does such an approach say about governmental respect for personal liberties?

In a particularly telling segment of the CBC video, a New Westminster sergeant in charge of the detail was asked whether he thought the enforcement efforts of his officers violated the rights of any of the people they were targeting. After contemplating his response for a moment, he replied that he had a right to live in a city that was safe and crime-free. From this standpoint, he continued, his rights superseded their rights. On the one hand, his comments are appealing to citizens weary of seeing their community overrun by crime and disorder. On the other, they are frightening because it is not up to the police to decide which—or whose—rights they will safeguard.

No responsible citizen would argue that driving crack dealers out of the community is a bad thing to do. Much to the contrary. All would agree that ridding the city of drugs and associated crime is a good thing and a very good end. In efforts such as those in New Westminster, though, deep and troubling questions remain about the way in which those positive outcomes are achieved. This is the classic tension confronting the police in a democracy: doing what must be done within the confines of the Constitution and the U.S. Bill of Rights (or the Canadian Charter of Rights). And sometimes—in fact, often—this makes the job of a police officer very difficult.

An additional complication for the police as they go about their work is the direction they receive from citizens in the community. The Canadian news media's broadcasting of the story about the New Westminster police brought the expected wave of criticism from some of the more liberal segments of society. But there was another interesting outpouring of citizen feedback as well. As soon as the CBC videos aired, the newspapers in New Westminster were inundated with letters to the editor, virtually all of them in praise of the police and critical of the media. In short, the message embodied in the overwhelming response from taxpayers in New Westminster was "Get off the backs of the police. They've done a wonderful job." New Westminster happens to be a Canadian city, but there are identical pressures on the police in the United States (and other democratic nations) as well.

In his investigation of the Rampart Division scandal in the Los Angeles Police Department, Lou Cannon interviewed a number of people living in the neighborhood who bluntly stated they were far more worried about the problems associated with gang activity than about police misconduct (*New York Times*, October 1, 2000). As one resident put it, "People have to make a choice, and most residents fear the gangs more than the police."

Regardless of where these issues arise, for the most part, all this talk about citizen rights and police practices makes interesting fodder for an intellectual discussion, without having any real meaning for law enforcement officers. In the minds of many street cops, it all boils down to a very simple issue: People simply don't understand or appreciate what police officers do. As evidence, a survey in the New York City Police Department in 1994 indicated that officers overwhelmingly believed the public does not understand the problems of police officers and, furthermore, won't support them (see Table 2.1).

The same survey, which included a series of questions about levels of trust and understanding within the police organization itself, revealed significant differences between what police officers saw as the most important part of their jobs and what they believed the department wanted most from them. From the point

TABLE 2.1   Understanding and Supporting the Police

	RESPONDENTS WHO	
	AGREE	DISAGREE
The public has no understanding of police problems.	90.8%	7.0%
The community has a good relationship with the police.	23.0%	74.5%
The public believes the police use too much force.	81.4%	16.2%
The media help the police do their jobs.	15.0%	82.4%

TABLE 2.2   Just Doing My Job

CONSIDERED BY OFFICERS AS MOST IMPORTANT TO THE DEPARTMENT	CONSIDERED BY OFFICERS AS MOST IMPORTANT TO THEMSELVES
1. Write summonses.	1. Reduce crime, disorder, and fear.
2. Hold down overtime.	2. Make gun arrests.
3. Stay out of trouble.	3. Provide police services to people who request them.
4. Clear backlog of radio runs.	4. Gain public confidence in police integrity.
5. Report police corruption.	5. Arrest drug dealers.
6. Treat bosses with deference.	6. Correct quality-of-life conditions.
7. Reduce crime, disorder, and fear.	7. Stay out of trouble.

of view of line officers, in other words, not only the general public but also the department itself lacks an understanding of what they do (see Table 2.2).

IN SEARCH OF "JUSTICE"

In their book *Police Ethics: The Corruption of Noble Cause* (2000), Michael Caldero and John Crank provide an incisive overview of the fundamental tension in doing the good work that police officers do. And although a number of things may draw a person to a career in law enforcement, Caldero and Crank point out that very often one of the most powerful is a belief in the inherent goodness (the "noble cause") of what police officers do for a living. Police officers believe themselves to be keepers of the peace, defenders of those unable to defend themselves, and the "thin line between civilization and anarchy."

But trying to do the good work of policing can be a frustrating experience. Many street police officers look on their department leaders and the criminal justice system as impediments to the important work of "getting the bad guy." Rules, court decisions, and constitutional limits all combine to complicate the life of a street cop. As a consequence, officers sometimes develop strategies for smoothing off the rough spots to make the system work more effectively. There is an old joke about the manner in which police officers sometimes "bend the rules" in order to close a case. (I will use the New York Police Department [NYPD] in the joke, although you could substitute any agency.)

> In an effort to determine the top crime-fighting agency in the country, the president narrowed the field to three final-ists: the CIA, the FBI, and the New York City Police Depart-ment. These three contenders were assigned the task of finding and catching a rabbit that had been released into the forest.
>
> The CIA went into the forest. Agents placed informants throughout. They questioned all plant and mineral witnesses. After three months of extensive investigation, they concluded that rabbits do not exist.
>
> The FBI went into the forest. After two weeks without a cap-ture, agents burned the forest, killing everything in it, including the rabbit. They made no apologies. The rabbit deserved it.
>
> The New York City Police Department went into the forest. Officers came out two hours later with a badly beaten bear. The bear was yelling "Okay, okay, I'm a rabbit, I'm a rabbit."

Consider another hypothetical—but more realistic—dilemma. This one involves a police officer who makes a traffic stop and finds a large quantity of drugs in the vehicle. He has the evidence of a crime, and he has the bad guy who did it, but there is a problem: The contraband was found locked in a sealed container in the trunk. Under the rules of search and seizure, he knows he had no author-ity to open the trunk and container, and it is clear that if he testifies truthfully about the manner in which the drugs were found, they will never be admitted into evidence. For some, this kind of problem is easily solved by testifying that the contraband was seen protrud-ing from beneath the front seat of the vehicle, thereby making it admissible under the plain-view doctrine. In other words, lying. In such cases, the false testimony is rationalized by the argument that drugs are evil and the motorist who possessed them is a bad guy. In the minds of some officers, it is sometimes necessary to bend the rules to "do the right thing."

In the Rampart Division of the Los Angeles Police Department, the issue of "bending the rules" was not hypothetical; it was reality. In an interview by Cannon published in the *New York Times* (October 1, 2000, p. 36) disgraced police officer Rafael Perez left no doubt that he was completely at ease when he lied to put gang members in jail. "These guys don't play by the rules; we don't have to play by the rules," he said. "They're out there committing murders and then they intimidate the witnesses, so the witnesses don't show up in court. So they're getting away with murder every day." From Perez's point of view, he took the actions he did to even the score. "When I planted a case on someone, did I feel bad?" he asked. "Not once. I felt good. I felt, you know, I'm taking this guy off the streets."

Prior to being disbanded in 2002, the Street Crime Unit (SCU) in the New York Police Department (more about them in Chapter 5) had a well-deserved reputation for effectiveness and efficiency in the battle to remove illegal firearms from the streets of that city. In the last couple of years of its existence, in fact, that small, highly motivated, and extraordinarily aggressive team was responsible for approximately 40 percent of the total number of gun arrests made by the entire police department. Unfortunately, almost one-half of those criminally charged by the SCU with possessing an illegal firearm never saw the inside of a courtroom because county district attorneys chose not to prosecute their cases. The reason? A lack of probable cause for arrest. When asked about the high number of cases being dismissed for what amounted to constitutional reasons (Fourth Amendment protection against "unreasonable search and seizure"), one SCU commander said he was not concerned. In his view, the mission of the SCU was, first and foremost, to remove illegal guns from the street, and decisions about whether or not to prosecute were made elsewhere. As he said, simply getting the guns off the street was, in itself, a laudatory accomplishment, for a gun off the street is not going to be involved in a robbery.

Similarly, the New Jersey State Police, in the 1980s and 1990s, had developed the science of highway drug interdiction into a virtual art form. Woe be to drug smugglers (or even private citizens, for that matter) traveling northbound on I-95 into the state of New Jersey, for after passing through the toll barrier that demarks the southern end of the New Jersey Turnpike, they unknowingly entered an area widely known as "Cocaine Alley." In that vicinity,

New Jersey troopers habitually parked in the highway median and scanned northbound traffic for vehicles they thought might be involved in the transportation of illegal drugs. When a trooper spotted a vehicle he thought might warrant scrutiny, he would execute a traffic stop and proceed through one or another of the various steps involved in a drug interdiction search.

As a result of their efforts, New Jersey troopers earned wide acclaim for their bounteous seizures of drugs and associated contraband from motorists using highways in their state. But like their counterparts with the NYPD Street Crime Unit, troopers in the Garden State had difficulty with the Fourth Amendment to the U.S. Constitution (prohibiting unreasonable search and seizure), causing many of their drug arrests to be thrown out of court for lack of any probable cause. When asked about this disparity between arrests resulting in the seizure of contraband and subsequent prosecution of those charged, one state police sergeant actively involved in the drug interdiction initiative responded dismissively: "Our job is to get the drugs off the street, not to worry about prosecutions."

HONESTY, INTEGRITY, AND "TESTILYING"

The noted criminal defense attorney and television personality Alan Dershowitz must have been amazed several years ago at the company in which he found himself. In a discussion about the darker side of the police culture in the United States, he noted that in his experience it was not unusual for police officers to engage in a practice known as "testilying." He went on to define the practice as one in which police testimony would be tailored to fit the elements of a particular offense or to comply with a particular legal requirement. Normally such a provocative statement would evoke howls of outrage from police leaders, union representatives, and others, but this time their protest was somewhat muted by the fact that Dershowitz's opinion was echoed by none other than Bill Bratton, police chief in Los Angeles, and Ray Kelley, police commissioner in New York City.

Testilying 101 will never be found on the schedule of courses taught at the local police academy; it is never presented in such forthright fashion. Instead, the practice is learned, honed, and passed on in other less formal (but likely more effective) ways. For example, officers seeking a search warrant based on the work of a confidential informant know they must be prepared to convince the issuing magistrate of the past reliability of the informant; this is no small task, since the informant is likely also involved in the drug trade. Agents of the U.S. Drug Enforcement Administration (DEA) found themselves struggling with this exact dilemma in the late 1990s, as they fought to defend their continued use of one particularly well-paid superinformant to make criminal cases against key figures in the drug trade. The issue was complicated by the fact that the DEA knew the informant had testified falsely (perjured himself) on several occasions about his criminal history, a fact that served to open more than one hundred felony convictions to challenge.

Sometimes the lessons given young officers leave no doubt about what is expected of them in putting together a defensible criminal case. Consider, for example, the young trooper who activated his emergency lights one evening to pull over a car for speeding. It turned out to be an interesting traffic stop because as soon as the violator saw the emergency lights in his rearview mirror, he threw a number of items (hash pipes, roach clips, and bags of marijuana) out the window of his vehicle. Much of the contraband bounced off the hood and windshield of the young officer's patrol car, so after stopping the violator on the shoulder of the road and taking the citizen's keys, he walked back up the road, picked up the drugs and paraphernalia, and then arrested the driver for speeding and criminal possession of the items he had tossed onto the highway.

Later, back at the station, the young trooper was describing the circumstances of the arrest when an older officer asked a piercing question: "How do you know the items you picked up came from the car you were stopping?" The young officer said, "Well, I saw them come out of the window of his car and they bounced off my car." The other officer then repeated: "No, how do you know *those* items came from *that* car?" The blood immediately drained from the young officer's face, as he realized he had not considered the possibility that the items he retrieved as evidence might not have been the right ones. Since it was dark at the time of the traffic stop, it was entirely possible the items he had picked up were already lying there, with the ones actually thrown from the car still scattered elsewhere along the roadway. The young officer knew his case was doomed because any judge would recognize the obvious problem with the chain of evidence.

The senior officer smiled reassuringly and said, "Let me tell you how you knew those were the items that came from the car you were stopping." He then suggested that the young trooper indicate in his report that at the time of the traffic stop, the driver's window on the patrol vehicle was rolled all the way down. "Then," he continued, "when the items were thrown out onto the pavement, you took one of your gloves off the seat of your car and you threw it out on the road as well. That way, after you secured the violator's vehicle, you were able to walk back, find your glove, and pick up the drug paraphernalia located all around it." When you report it this way, the senior man concluded, there is never a problem with getting evidence admitted into court. The message was clear: You have the evidence, you have the bad guy, and now we just have to make the facts fit together the way they should.

Putting aside the outrageous and high-profile scandals we see repeated ad nauseam across every television channel, it is important to remember that, for the most part, police officers are good people who do an extremely difficult job and do it well. When they "bend the rules" in the course of doing their jobs, it is rarely for personal gain or aggrandizement. Rather, it is typically because they have an inherent sense of right and wrong and want to help those who cannot defend themselves. Caldero and Crank (2000, p. 35) refer to this attribute as "the smell of the victim's blood," meaning that police officers feel a powerful sense of obligation to balance things when someone has been injured or deprived of rights or property. In his article titled "Why Cops Hate You" (1986), Chuck Milland made the point this way:

> Probably the most serious beef cops have with civilians relates to those situations in which the use of force becomes necessary to deal with some desperado who may have just robbed a bank, iced somebody, beat up his wife and kids, or wounded some cop, and now he's caught, but won't give up. He's not going to be taken alive, he's going to take some cops with him, and you better say your prayers, you pig bastards! Naturally, if the chump's armed with any kind of weapon, the cops are going to shoot the shit out of him so bad they'll be able to open up his body later as a lead mine. If he's not armed, and the cops aren't creative enough to find a weapon for him, they'll just beat him into raw meat and hope he spends the next few weeks in traction. They view it as a learning experience for the a**hole. You f**k up somebody, you find out what it feels

like to get f**ked up. Don't like it? Don't do it again! It's called "street justice," and civilians approve of it as much as cops do—even if they don't admit it.

Remember how the audience cheered when Charles Bronson f**ked up the bad guys in *Death Wish*? How they scream with joy every time Clint Eastwood's Dirty Harry makes his day by blowing up some rotten scumball with his .44 Magnum? What they applaud is the administration of street justice. The old eye-for-an-eye concept, one of mankind's most primal instincts. All of us have it, especially cops. (p. 50)

The well-known comedian Dennis Miller reminds us of how fortunate we are to have police officers willing to do what they do and how appreciative we should be that they are around when we most need them. He puts his observations this way:

And for all you ACLU members out there without A-C-L-U-E: When you hear a noise outside your house in the middle of the night and you fear for your life and call 911, just be glad it's cops who show up at your front door and not Alan Dershowitz, because believe me, if it was Dershowitz, you'd end up . . .

Well, let's leave it at that. When you call, the police will come. And when they get there, they will protect you.

DISCUSSION QUESTIONS

1. In New Westminster, British Columbia, citizens spoke out in support of the strategies their police employed to rid the community of drug dealers. What factors might have provoked a different reaction in the community?

2. As long as the police are doing a good job (as measured by arrest statistics and a low crime rate), how concerned should law-abiding citizens be about the tactics used to achieve that success?

3. If a police officer searches a vehicle without justification and then arrests the driver for possession of a small amount of marijuana, is it acceptable for him to testify falsely about how he recovered the evidence? Remember, the evidence will be excluded (and the arrest voided) if the search was improper.

4. If that same unjustified search resulted in the recovery of evidence linking the driver to a series of brutal sexual assaults, would your answer be the same? Why or why not?

chapter 3

THE CULTURE
OF POLICING

To the Citizen: As you read this chapter, bring to mind a few of the outward characteristics or traits that uniformed police officers seem to have in common. How do they make you feel? What message do they send? Do other professions have cultures of their own? What are the benefits of a professional culture? What are the drawbacks?

To the Police Officer: Before reading this chapter, bring to mind a few of the obvious outward characteristics that uniformed police officers seem to have in common. Once you have done so, consider the way someone outside the police community might perceive them. Are there ways in which the police separate themselves from other people? What are they? If there is a culture of policing, how is it passed from one generation to the next?

According to *Webster's Dictionary*, one definition of culture is "the customary beliefs, social forms, and material traits of a racial, religious, or social group." In other words, the way people walk, communicate, or dress—to name just a few characteristics—will serve to join together the members of one particular group and differentiate it from another. This observation will not come as a surprise to experienced law enforcement officers, by the way, because they understand and appreciate the strength and durability of the police culture.

THE POWER OF THE POLICE CULTURE

For those who doubt whether the law enforcement profession separates police officers from others in the community, consider a simple question: What other group of workers begins the day by putting on clothing that distinguishes them from everyone else in the community, getting into gaudily painted automobiles with lots of lights on top, and then riding around town "looking for trouble"? When police officers walk along the street, even their gait and posture are distinctive. Officers would call it "confident" or "self-assured"; citizens, on the other hand, often describe it as "arrogant" or "cocky." Sometimes even the language police officers use to communicate with one another has a special flair that only other cops can understand and decipher. What is a "camp follower"? Or a "skell"? Or "collars for dollars"?

The notion of a police culture, though, goes even deeper than the outward symbols that can be observed and measured. In the law enforcement community, *culture* can be described as an invisible style or a way of doing business that in many ways is more powerful than the rules and regulations of a police department. In reality, it is the unwritten guide to "how we do things around here." The police culture provides meaning and direction to officers and has the effect of shaping, driving, and sustaining the group's choices and actions. It is a force field of energy with an existence and life all its own, and often it is entirely separate from the organization's mission, rewards systems, policies, and job descriptions. Ultimately, it is the force that controls members' behaviors and attitudes in the workplace. And for a law enforcement officer, this can be both good and bad.

Depending on a variety of factors, individual citizens characterize the profession of law enforcement in very different ways. Even police officers, at various times over the course of their careers, will likely use very different words to describe the work they do and their relationships with the agencies that employ them. But as they discuss and occasionally complain about "the job," cops universally tend to speak with great reverence about one omnipresent professional value: loyalty. And this makes perfect sense, for the difficult, dangerous, complex work of policing frequently places officers in situations in which they have to depend on one another in the extreme. Sometimes they depend on each other for the very protection of life and limb. As a result, the camaraderie and trust of street policing tend to foster the development of very powerful and intimate bonds. Unfortunately, these bonds, when subverted, sometimes result in confusion about what loyalty really means.

For example, police officers have an absolute right to expect backup (physical assistance) from other officers in times of need. And most police officers understand this expectation; even the least popular officer on a squad knows that when he or she calls for help, it will arrive quickly and in force. The backup patrols may not converse with the officer or offer to go for coffee afterward, but they will swoop in and bail him or her out with no questions asked. There are exceptions to this rule, as we shall see, but unquestioned loyalty in the context of physical assistance is generally understood by all to transcend any personality differences or tensions that might exist among officers. This type of loyalty is a credit to those who police the streets.

But the notion of loyalty quickly becomes an embarrassment and a liability to policing when it is misunderstood and misused. When this happens, the term *loyalty* sometimes becomes synonymous with *lie* or *cover-up*. In other words, cops who have engaged in wrongdoing sometimes expect other officers to fabricate stories or withhold information to protect them. For example, in August 1997, Abner Louima, a Haitian immigrant, was physically tortured by several members of the New York City Police Department (NYPD) while in their custody. Speaking shortly after this incident, New York Mayor Rudy Giuliani noted that while most police officers would never consider engaging in such a wholly despicable act (Louima had been anally sodomized with a wooden stick), he was dismayed that other police officers who saw or knew about it did not step forward to prevent or report it. Why, he wondered, would people remain silent in the face of such a horrific offense?

Giuliani was expressing his dismay at the well-documented and much-discussed law enforcement "code of silence." There can be little doubt that such a thing exists in the law enforcement community, but it is not a phenomenon rooted solely in the rank and file of a police agency. According to an article in the *Los Angeles Times* (August 26, 2000), more than forty current and former Los Angeles Police Department (LAPD) officers filed a class-action lawsuit alleging that commanders in the agency support a code of silence, as demonstrated by their retaliation against those who report misconduct. When one officer said in a court deposition that the shooting of a mentally ill homeless woman was unwarranted, for example, his testimony resulted in a departmental investigation of him. In 1999 Los Angeles city officials passed a law forbidding retaliation against employees who file complaints with the police commission, but many officers remain convinced they will face retaliation if they report misconduct by another officer.

As the sordid details of the Rampart scandal in the LAPD continued to surface in 1999 and 2000, there emerged a breathtaking example of leadership behavior that many would say fed into and strengthened a corrupt culture. According to a reporter for the *Los Angeles Times*, some sergeants in charge of antigang units in that division made it a practice to award plaques to officers who were involved in a shooting incident. Arrayed on each plaque were playing cards that, in poker, would comprise the "dead man's hand" (aces and eights). If the officer had been involved in a shooting that resulted in someone only being wounded, the cards on his plaque were red (hearts and diamonds). If the shooting incident resulted in a fatality, the officer received a plaque with black cards (spades and clubs).

THE RODNEY KING INCIDENT

Although the infamous Rodney King video is now more than ten years old (the event happened on March 3, 1991), it remains a useful tool for discussion of concepts such as loyalty among street cops and respect for citizens. In a classroom full of police officers, it is always interesting to record the answers to the simple question, "Why didn't some of the twenty-six officers circled around the Rodney King altercation step forward and say that's enough . . . that's excessive?" There are usually a number of different responses, including the following:

There was a sergeant on the scene, and he was in charge.
Officers at the scene did not know all the details.
It was somebody else's arrest. It was none of my business.
The guy was a scumbag, and he deserved what he got.

But there are two other more frequently voiced responses that stand out. The first speculates that officers may not have stepped forward simply because they saw nothing out of the ordinary. The second—and overall most powerful—is peer pressure.

It is amazing to consider that someone could be at the scene of the Rodney King incident (or watch it on video) and conclude that there was nothing extraordinary in the police behavior occurring there. To hold to this point of view is to say that the officers' actions recorded that day were simply "how we do business around here." If this is the case, then it is possible to understand how the officers who were watching from the perimeter may have become inured to what they were seeing and therefore felt no need to intercede or report the incident. And, besides, any officer at that scene uneasy about what went on knew better than to step forward because, in that environment, there was no confusion about what the costs of breaking away from the crowd would be. The officer would have been ostracized.

Some police officers scoff at the suggestion that cops who break the bond of loyalty run the risk of not receiving backup, but an incident in New York City in April 2000 demonstrates otherwise. According to a report in the *New York Times* by Flynn (April 4, 2000), a female NYPD police officer assigned to the 83rd precinct was driving home from a party when she struck several parked cars in the 104th precinct (the 104th is located, incidentally, in an entirely different borough of New York City from the 83rd). Officers from the 104th responded to the accident and, after noting that she appeared to have been drinking, arrested the female officer for driving while intoxicated. At the end of the shift that morning, three officers from the arrested officer's precinct—in uniform and in a marked patrol unit—drove to the 104th precinct (remember, in another borough), entered the locker room, and berated the officer who had earlier arrested their colleague. Their rebuke included the warning that he "should not expect backup from anyone in the 83rd precinct" and concluded with the warning that it would be wise for him to "watch [his] back because [he] might catch a bullet."

When it comes to the issue of problem police officers in the ranks of law enforcement, the very real power of the police culture becomes evident. It surfaces in the coping strategies officers use to avoid working with some of their peers, because most cops know which of their coworkers have reputations for corrupt or assaultive behavior. And this is where the tension lies; although they may personally avoid partnering with a problem officer, they are reluctant to step forward and report the scoundrel through official channels. Seldom is this practice more evident than in those instances when corrupt cops are finally charged and dismissed from the force. Their dismissal often brings an almost audible sigh of relief from their peers, followed by the remark "It's about time they caught up with them."

This is a very difficult discussion for law enforcement professionals. In fact, when it is suggested that police officers should be more willing to report corrupt or criminal actions by their peers, someone always makes the point that doctors and lawyers do not readily report misbehavior by their professional colleagues either. True enough. But when it comes to policing, the notion of the public trust makes a significant difference. We, as citizens, vest enormous power and authority in police officers, going so far as to give up our right to enforce our rights; we have entrusted this duty, instead, to the police in the communities where we reside. In return, there is a legitimate expectation that police power and authority will be used responsibly, fairly, and equitably at all times and under all circumstances.

Across the police profession on an international level, there is a phenomenon that is generally unknown and invisible to outsiders but clearly acknowledged and understood by those on the inside. It has to do with police officers' deeply held view that other police officers are "family," extending to the belief that when the chips are down, the only people who can be relied on to stand up and protect a cop are other cops. Paranoid though this perspective may seem, police officers see ample evidence in the way the media portray them and politicians cut them loose during difficult times. Consequently, many cops develop a highly insular view of themselves, with an almost universal tendency to separate society into two very distinct groups. The first of these groups is the police themselves; the second is everyone else.

But for many police officers, a mere acknowledgment of this separation is inadequate. Instead, they choose to outline the depths of the abyss through the use of an extensive menu of offensive words and phrases to characterize noncops. It would be interesting to collect and catalogue the assortment of terms officers routinely employ to describe others, but any attempt to do so would be doomed to fail for at least three reasons. First, such an inventory could never include all the current nomenclature; the list would be far too long, and there is a risk that somewhere a group of police officers would be offended that the highly imaginative and colorful colloquialism they had coined was overlooked. Second, most citizens would never believe that police officers actually use these kinds of words and phrases to describe them. And third, no editor or censor would ever permit such a list to appear in print. Nor should they. Suffice it to say that the jargon employed by police officers to describe people in the "other" group is not ordinarily repeated in polite company.

Joseph Wambaugh, the renowned Los Angeles police detective and writer, gives the reader a vivid and highly accurate look at this phenomenon in his book *The Choirboys* (1975). In this classic fiction-based-on-fact work, he relates a conversation among a group of imaginary LAPD officers at a party (or "choir practice") after work one night. One of them in particular, a rogue officer named Roscoe Rules, was trying to come up with a sufficiently derogatory name for citizens, but the right word continued to elude him. Ever helpful, his intoxicated fellow officers began to make suggestions, at which point the reader is treated to an amazingly creative string of epithets, expletives, and bizarre references to various body parts. Wambaugh's passage finally concludes with a self-satisfied Roscoe crafting a term that, in his mind, successfully blended his disdain for the general public with a suitably offensive anatomical reference.

Whether intended or not, the description of Roscoe Rules's dilemma makes a powerful point about the division between the police and others in society. If you doubt such a division exists, ask a group of citizens to read the list of outlandish words and phrases Wambaugh suggests officers routinely use to describe members of the general public. Next, ask a group of police officers to read the same list. Be sure to carefully note the reactions of both groups. In most cases citizens will be repulsed; police officers, though, will laugh openly.

Nowhere is this phenomenon more noticeable than in a classroom full of in-service police officers talking about police-community relations. To stimulate discussion, instructors may ask the group whether Wambaugh-like lists of noncop descriptors exist and then go so far as to list some for consideration. The terms are always met with a great deal of laughter and knowing nods (and officers often suggest others the instructor might have overlooked). But it is important to remember that even though this discussion serves as a lighthearted way of looking at the issue, what it really describes is a virtually impenetrable wall between the police and everyone else in society. For cops, it is another way of confirming a fact they know to be true: The only person you can trust and honestly communicate with is another police officer.

It is important to stop for a moment and acknowledge that some police officers reading this description may object to the outline of the cops and noncops phenomenon, arguing that the condition is not nearly as pervasive as represented. But the fact is, most cops—at least in their hearts—will know exactly what I am talking about here. And even if they happen to rise above it, they know many other officers who absolutely divide humanity along these basic lines. This is not to say that every police officer uses profane or offensive terms when referring to citizens, at least not at the start of a career. The process by which cops place noncops in that "other" category is typically incremental in nature, often reflecting a gradual creep of cynicism into a law enforcement personality.

POLICING AND THE "SEVEN VEILS"

In the Bible there is an account of a young woman who danced for Herod, and though she was not identified and the dance was not described, it reports that Herod "was moved." In 1905 Richard Strauss built his opera *Salomé* on that biblical story, introducing Western society to a young woman (the namesake of the opera) and her exotic dance. The dance, known as the Dance of the Seven Veils, had Salomé slowly peel away veils one at a time, thereby becoming gradually more visible to Herod.

Police officers do much the same thing, but in precisely the opposite fashion. Rather than removing veils as Salomé did, over the course of their careers police officers tend to place veils between themselves and various other groups of people and individuals. It happens incrementally, but as officers find themselves looking at people through an increasing number of veils, the features of those on the other side gradually become less distinct. Ultimately, this large community of noncops simply becomes one amorphous mass. And as they fall into place one by one, these veils become a solid curtain—a "blue curtain"—and officers find themselves on one side and virtually everyone else on the other.

Let me explain how the process works. Shortly after a police officer is sworn in and goes out on the street for the first time, it becomes evident that there are some very bad people in the world. These are people who commit serious violations of law and crimes of violence. A police officer knows he is not one of them—they are, after all, "bad guys" and he is one of the "good guys"—so the first veil drops into place as he separates himself from criminals and other desperados.

Not long afterward, the police officer begins to notice that a lot of other people—speeders and people who commit other similarly benign infractions, for example—belong on the other side of the curtain as well. An officer knows he is looking through that second veil when he hears himself saying things like "52 miles per hour in a 35-mile-per-hour zone . . . what an [expletive deleted]."

The third veil falls into place when the officer reaches a conclusion that he knows to be true: that everyone except police officers are clearly different from him and therefore among this "other" group. The first indication that an officer has arrived at this level often comes at a social gathering where people are talking about what they do for a living. After somebody in the group mentions that he works for IBM, for example, the officer will know he is peering through one more veil when he finds himself turning to his companion and whispering, "IBM . . . nothing but idiots and lowlifes work at IBM."

It doesn't take much longer for the officer to arrive at the next irrefutable truth: that everybody with the rank of sergeant or above has lost any connection with the reality of life on the street. Consequently, since these bosses (even though they are cops) have forgotten what "real" police work is like, they are no different from all the "others," and the fourth veil drops. The officer is judicious as he voices his concerns about how out of touch his supervisors are, of course, but when he is among his peers out on patrol discussing a new policy developed by the command staff, he can't help but wonder "what those clowns up in the puzzle palace could possibly be thinking."

As time goes on, veil number five gradually drifts into place. This happens when the officer realizes that, in his mind, the only real police work in his department is being done by people on his own shift; everyone else is just taking up space and wasting time. And as far as he is concerned, the people working day shift are particularly suspect. "What," he wonders, "do those losers working the day shift do out there anyway?"

When the sixth veil falls into position, the officer is suddenly struck by the realization that the only people who are still free from the taint of association with that "other" group are he and his patrol partner. But as he begins to think about it (here comes the seventh veil), even his partner has been acting kind of strange lately.

At the end of a classroom session exploring the process by which officers separate themselves from others in society, it is interesting to watch what happens when the instructor announces, "I need five volunteers to step forward to help with an exercise to prove something." Nobody ever steps forward from the group, of course, and this is the point of the exercise: that nobody will step forward. When the instructor asks why nobody volunteered, the responses range from a laughing "I didn't want to be seen as one of those lowlife citizens we just finished talking about" to comments about limited information concerning the exercise and the consequent fear of the unknown. The point is, of course, it is very difficult to step away from a comfortable group and into a situation in which you are unsure of what is going to happen.

As mentioned in the earlier discussion of the Rodney King event, peer pressure in the world of street policing is more than just a topic for intellectual examination. To police officers, it is intertwined with the notion of loyalty, and while it may be difficult to put the exact definition into words, there is no mistaking what it means to a cop at gut level. It means physical safety. In other words, officers know that if they violate the loyalty of the street by speaking out about misbehavior, they run the risk of not getting backup from their peers at some point down the road.

Most police officers, at one time or another in their careers, have been involved in a high-speed chase in pursuit of a fleeing vehicle. Once you have been there, you don't soon forget the experience—heavy adrenalin dump, blood pressure off the chart, anger, excitement, and, yes, fear as well. When pressed, officers acknowledge that at times like these, an officer can be "walking on the edge of the envelope" in terms of self-control. In these circumstances, then, the term *backup* can mean more than simply arriving at the scene in force with more weapons or manpower; *backup* can mean arriving with a cooler head. It can mean interceding for an officer who is out of control and taking over the scene while he has a chance to calm down.

That being the case, one could argue that the officers standing in the circle around the Rodney King beating did not back up the four officers who were most directly involved. Instead, they left them out there to swing, both literally and figuratively.

In discussing the depth and breadth of the law enforcement culture, attention is most often given to the negative things that result from a corrupt or otherwise unhappy environment. But the often overlooked fact is that many positive and productive benefits flow from a healthy police culture. For one thing, officers who as a group are generally warm, caring, and upright individuals find themselves connected in an almost mystical fashion to the bulk of other like members of the profession around the world. When police officers from the United States travel to Europe, for example, all they have to do is identify themselves to officers in the country they are visiting and they will be met with open arms. Doors will be opened, spare bedrooms will become available, meals will be provided and taken with other officers, all in the name of the shared experience of policing and regardless of the jurisdiction.

Critics frequently describe and complain of a secretive, insular world of policing, and they have a point. But officers have a tendency to close around one another in very positive ways as well. When an officer is injured or in need of medical assistance, for example, other cops show up from all over the city and many other jurisdictions to donate blood or provide support to the fallen colleague and his family. And whenever an off-duty police officer sees an on-duty officer make a traffic stop, she will always slow down to make sure everything is under control. She will do so even with her family in the car and traveling in another state because she knows the next time she is stopping a traffic violator in her own jurisdiction, any off-duty officer who happens to be passing by will do exactly the same thing for her.

PASSING ALONG THE CULTURE OF POLICING

In their book *The Power of Ethical Management*, Ken Blanchard and Norman Vincent Peale (1996) discuss the manner in which each of us learns how we ought to behave in certain circumstances or social situations. In their typically succinct fashion, they describe the process in this way:

Our values are primarily caught, not taught. (p. 74)

Applying this observation to the field of law enforcement makes a lot of trainers, administrators, and department leaders very nervous because it raises significant doubts about the effects of formal classroom training, particularly as it relates to the development of new employees. What it says, in effect, is that much of the good, dedicated, policy-driven educational experience a new recruit officer receives in an academic setting can be negated in short order by a street culture that condones (or even requires) corrupt behavior. Take, for example, the young officer who spends the final two weeks of the police academy deeply immersed in a discussion of ethics, including the identification and analysis of moral dilemmas and the study of ethics decision-making models. What is likely to happen if, at the end of that two-week classroom experience, she graduates and is assigned to a corrupt patrol partner who sees ethics as an impediment? There are no guarantees, of course, but it is likely her academic discussion and examination of ethics will succumb to the real-world experience she is surrounded by, immersed in, and continually exposed to out on the street.

Recruit police officers learn a number of things in the police academy, and they learn them in a variety of ways. But when it comes to imparting information to trainees about the parameters and protocol of the police culture, few lessons can compare to the one taught at the New York City Police Academy (*New York Times*, August 8, 1995, p. 22) in the summer of 1995 (see box on pages 40–41).

In much the same way as law enforcement agencies select and hire new employees, corrupt police subcultures screen new candidates as well. For instance, when Michael Dowd was trying to determine whether a particular officer might be suitable for inclusion in his group of dishonest colleagues in the 1990s in New York City, he would subject him to a series of gradually more detailed tests. First, the officer might be asked to violate a minor departmental rule such as leaving his patrol post without permission. Next, he might be given the opportunity to drink a beer while on duty or to accept free food, in violation of NYPD policy. Once satisfied that the officer could be "trusted," Dowd might then invite him to participate in some of the nefarious behavior for which he and many of his colleagues were eventually convicted and incarcerated.

One of Michael Dowd's former cohorts, Bernard Cawley, was sentenced to prison for crimes he committed while a New York

NEW YORK'S SURLIEST

The lessons in vindictiveness start early in the New York City Police Department. Just ask the Zanikos family, which runs a restaurant patronized by police recruits but now finds itself the target of a boycott after one of them spoke the truth to a reporter about police behavior.

The story began when the *Times* columnist Joyce Purnick was preparing an article on illegal parking by police officers throughout the city. She interviewed Peter Zanikos, whose family restaurant, Michelle's, is around the corner from the police academy and caters mainly to its instructors and recruits. Mr. Zanikos made the mistake of asking two common rhetorical questions posed by many citizens who see police cars parked in defiance of the law: "Why don't cops put a quarter in the meter like I do? Why don't they get tickets like I do?"

Ms. Purnick quoted Mr. Zanikos in her column on June 22. In the meantime, Mr. Zanikos threw a party for the latest class's graduation. That was the sort of relationship he had with the recruits. They were happy to come. Apparently they either had not read the column or did not take it seriously.

But then, late last month, someone made copies of the article and circulated it at the academy. Sergeants brought the article to the recruits' attention. Suddenly business went bad at the restaurant. Some days no police showed up. Last Friday five recruits broke ranks and went to Michelle's for lunch because smoking is allowed in a back room. Yesterday morning WINS broadcast a report on the restaurant's plight, giving its address. At lunchtime the place was full—but not one uniform. The clientele consisted entirely of sympathetic citizens.

A Patrolmen's Benevolent Association spokesman, Joseph Mancini, whose union backs the right to boycott businesses that "aren't treating cops properly," says it was not just remarks about illegal parking that upset the recruits. He said some of them felt the restaurant staff were not treating them with respect. He did not explain why the same recruits had attended the Zanikoses' party for them. He insisted that recruits were also put out with another business in the area, an equipment supply store, but he could not name the store.

This sort of episode can only confirm New Yorkers' worst fears about the culture of the city's Police Department. Police Commissioner William Bratton has struggled hard to break down the blue wall of silence when police have broken the law. Now he must contend with a class of recruits—and their instructors—who cannot even abide frank speech from a small-business man.

They are willing to destroy a family's livelihood to show that they will not tolerate criticism that every New Yorker knows is true. No wonder the N.Y.P.D. has such trouble policing itself. Right from the start, its recruits are taught that the police are above the law.

Commissioner Bratton cannot tell his officers where to eat. But he could set an example by dropping by Michelle's—and taking 20 or 30 of his closest friends in uniform.

City police officer. When he was brought from jail to testify before the Mollen Commission about some of his misdeeds, Cawley's stunning remarks detailed not only the extent to which he and his colleagues had misbehaved but the power (and comfort) of their group culture as well. In his testimony, Cawley easily described the assaults and other assorted crimes his clique engaged in, but he seemed momentarily confused when asked "Weren't you afraid of being caught?" After thinking about it for a moment, he replied simply, "No. Who was going to catch us? We were the police." In other words, he was completely at ease and immersed in the values of that out-of-control group, so much so that he *knew* none of his fellow members would ever turn him in . . . and he was right.

In May 2000, the U.S. Department of Justice (Weisburd and Greenspan) reported on a nationally representative telephone survey of 925 randomly selected American police officers from 121 departments who were asked to comment on the abuse of police authority. The report contains some interesting contradictions, including data showing that more than 80 percent of those surveyed said they do not accept the "code of silence" (remaining silent in the face of misconduct by others) as an essential part of the mutual trust necessary to good policing, while almost a quarter (24.9 percent) said that whistle-blowing is not worth it. In fact, more than two-thirds (67.4 percent) of those interviewed said that officers who report incidents of misconduct will likely receive the cold shoulder from fellow officers, and a majority (52.4 percent) said it is not unusual for police officers to turn a blind eye to other officers' misconduct. Finally, a surprising 61 percent of those surveyed said that police officers do not always report even serious criminal violations that involve the abuse of authority by fellow officers. Although we would like to chastise those officers who hold that blowing the whistle is "not worth it," they have a point. It does not take a great deal of effort to find examples of people in virtually every profession who stood up for what they thought was the right thing only to find themselves unfairly disciplined, shunned, and often driven from their organizations.

In their interim report addressing corruption within the New York City Police Department (December 27, 1993), the Mollen Commission entered a scathing observation about the power of a law enforcement culture:

> The code of silence and the "us versus them" mentality were present wherever we found corruption. These characteristics of police culture largely explain how groups of corrupt officers, sometimes comprising almost an entire squad, can openly engage in corruption for long periods of time with impunity. Any successful system for corruption control must redirect police culture against protecting and perpetuating police corruption. It must create a culture that demands integrity and works to ensure it. (p. 171)

Sometimes, police officers describe the police culture as something akin to a family, and that is a warm and comforting thought. On a chilly evening, a fire carefully set in a fireplace is warm and comforting as well. But a fire raging out of control is a dangerous and destructive thing, and so is a culture. As you continue to read this book, consider the impact the law enforcement culture might have on things such as officer safety, interactions with citizens from various racial and ethnic groups, and the ability of police organizations to investigate themselves.

DISCUSSION QUESTIONS

1. Is loyalty an important condition within the ranks of law enforcement? Why? Is it possible to identify the point at which loyalty becomes blind loyalty? What is the difference between the two?

2. Considering either the Rodney King or Abner Louima incident as an example, what factors or concerns might have prevented some police officers at the scene from stepping forward to intercede even when other officers engaged in clearly improper behavior?

3. Do you believe the phenomenon of the "seven veils" affects all police officers equally? What factors could influence the degree to which an officer withdraws from other groups in society?

4. If Blanchard and Peale are correct in asserting that "values are primarily caught, not taught," what does this say about the influence of the culture in a given police agency? What about the role of the field training officer in that regard? The leadership or command team?

chapter 4

OFFICER SAFETY

To the Citizen: Before reading this chapter, bring to mind (as best you can) some statistics about police officers killed and injured in the line of duty each year. Do you have any idea how many officers are affected across the country? In your state? In your community? Do police officers have a right to feel concerned about their safety both on and off duty? Do officer safety practices affect the way you see the police? Why?

To the Police Officer: As you read this chapter, consider whether your officer safety practices are similar to those described. Does the nature of your job have an impact on how you see and interact with the world both on- and off-duty? Street survival training is important in law enforcement. Are there other training topics you could add that might make you even safer? What are they?

Amazing grace. For someone who has never attended a police funeral, these words may not have much meaning. They are the title of a piece of religious music, of course, a popular hymn sung in churches of many denominations. But in the tight-knit world of policing, the mere mention of the words *amazing grace* evokes very deep and powerful emotions. For those who do not understand, no explanation will ever be possible; for police officers, no explanation is necessary.

Few public ceremonies are conducted with the solemn dignity of a police funeral. Representatives of other police agencies come—some from great distances—to grieve with and support the family and coworkers of the fallen officer. Highways are closed off. A motorcade is formed. Hundreds, sometimes thousands, of officers line the street and stand at attention. And then it happens. As the hearse arrives, a single bagpipe plays the haunting melody of "Amazing Grace." And that sound goes deep into the very soul of every person within earshot—so much so that from that point on, every time a law enforcement officer hears "Amazing Grace," he will associate it with police funerals he has attended.

Police funerals always seem to be held on cold days, but, if not cold, they are at least overcast. And given the vast number of people in attendance, when the procession arrives at the cemetery, there is always a long walk from the car to the proximity of the graveside service. The clergy speak a few final words, the flag is carefully folded and presented to the family, there is a twenty-one-gun salute, "Taps" is played—often with an echo—and the assembled ranks are dismissed. Afterward, on the long walk back to their cars, many officers, touched deeply and reflecting on the events of the day, renew a silent vow they have made many times over the course of their careers: *This . . . will . . . not . . . happen . . . to . . . me.*

TURNING ON THE "RADAR"

From the first physical training or defensive tactics class in the recruit academy, young police officers are made to understand the connection between being in good physical condition and keeping oneself safe. Staying in shape is good common sense for everyone, of course, but for cops there is the added dimension of possibly having to overcome physical resistance or subdue a combative individual being taken into custody. As a consequence, wise police officers keep their eyes and ears open—literally—to spot potentially threatening situations, deal with them effectively, and go home safely at the end of the tour.

The physical senses of a police officer scan the environment much like radar, and many officers find it very difficult to shut these sensors down, even when they are off duty. A female police officer from a midsized police department in Texas tells about the evening when she and her husband, who is also a police officer, went to a party at a friend's house. Upon approaching the front entrance, one of them knocked, after which they both instinctively executed the officer safety tactic of standing close to the wall on opposite sides of the door, just as they would if they were seeking admittance to a home where they had been called to settle a family dispute. In fact, she says with a laugh, they had moved to cover so well that when the host opened the door, he had a surprised look on his face because, at first, he could not see anyone on his porch.

Like that officer and her husband in Texas, a police sergeant from an agency in New York State—let's call him Tom Michaels—learned, much to his surprise, that he too kept his personal radar turned on at all times. As a trainer of new recruits, Michaels took pride in instilling his charges with a sense of professionalism and discipline, and they took careful note of the ways—some intentional and some unintentional—in which he did so. He learned of his unconscious habits for the first time at an informal recruit graduation party, when a group of rookies referred to him as Tom "The Blade" Michaels. As the young officers went on to explain, Michaels had an instinctive tendency to "blade" everyone he spoke to, regardless of the circumstances.

By way of explanation, "blading" describes the physical stance or posture assumed by an officer who may, for example, be interviewing someone on the street. The object of taking a bladed stance is to remain balanced and alert so that if the other person makes a threatening move, the officer will be prepared to counter it. When bladed, an officer is turned slightly sideways with the weapon side away from the citizen. If the officer is right-handed, his left foot is slightly forward, and his weight is distributed 70-30, meaning 70 percent on the rear foot and 30 percent on the front foot; his hands are free and kept at about the waist to lower chest level; and his eye contact is direct and unwavering. Finally, in this officer safety mode, the officer's verbal communication is typically in the form of short and easily understood commands or questions.

When the recruit officers at the party nicknamed him "The Blade," it came as a surprise to Tom Michaels. He took his training role very seriously and was shocked to learn that his inability to turn off his radar was so noticeable to people in normal business and social situations. And while he tried to make light of his new nickname, the rookie officers received a show of support from an unexpected source. Michaels's wife happened to be at the party that night as well, and she pointed out that he had unconsciously been blading her and their three young children around the house for years.

It is easy to poke fun at the way some police officers carry their officer safety skills to what some would call ridiculous extremes, but there is no denying that the job of law enforcement is dangerous work. And although we may chuckle at the off-duty officer out for dinner with his family who instinctively sits with his back to the wall and faces the door, we know that if gunshots are heard in the restaurant parking lot, the police officer will immediately rise and run *toward* the sound of the shooting, while everyone else runs in the other direction or seeks cover.

EQUIPMENT AND TRAINING

Fortunately, most police departments have come to understand the importance of investing time and money on protective gear and training so officers will be as safe as possible. For most street police officers, though, it is never enough.

A quick review of law enforcement publications reveals a plethora of equipment available for purchase, including armored vehicles, night-vision gear, Kevlar body armor, sophisticated firearms, and high-tech communications equipment. And since such officer safety items rank high on the wish list of every street police officer, people charged with overseeing department budgets have a very real dilemma. What government official, after all, wants to publicly oppose the purchase of police protective equipment and, in the process, be labeled as someone who values the bottom line more than the safety of law enforcement officers?

The same argument applies to training. A cursory examination of police training Web sites and the offerings of professional law enforcement training organizations shows a vast array of in-service law enforcement classes, with the majority leaning toward an emphasis on officer safety and protection. At the January 1999 conference of the American Society of Law Enforcement Trainers (ASLET) held in Albuquerque, New Mexico, for example, an attendee didn't have to look hard to find a training session focused on police officer survival. Course offerings included fifteen firearms programs; twenty-four defensive tactics, handcuffing, and baton use sessions; eight on survival research; and eight dedicated to managing the use of force. A total of sixteen courses targeted instructor development and management skills, but of the remaining twenty-two sessions, eight dealt with such topics as the trauma of law enforcement death, survival tactics for off-duty and plainclothes officers, and survival training and protective equipment needs geared specifically toward women officers. At this conference, incidentally, there was only one session dealing with law enforcement ethics and none with cultural diversity. Given the overall tone of available training sessions at the 1999 ASLET conference, then, it was not surprising that the keynote address on the first day was titled "The Bulletproof Mind: Psychological Preparation for Combat, Killing, and Death."

This is not to say, by the way, that police departments should do away with officer safety and street survival programs. Absolutely not. Providing every available resource to protect the physical well-being of law enforcement officers should be of utmost importance to practitioners and citizens alike. But the relentless exposure to training programs that would have officers believe they are in some constant form of warfare status is a problem. In fact, such programs sometimes make situations worse rather than better.

It is difficult to raise questions about the ubiquitous street survival programs available on the law enforcement training market because skepticism about their focus is sometimes interpreted as a lack of support for the police. But there may be merit in asking police agencies to examine what happens after officers have gone through an intense survival course. One major East Coast agency, for example, experienced a significant rise in citizen complaints after such training, apparently attributable, at least in part, to the increased tendency of officers to view *all* citizens as a threat. In fact, this is exactly the explanation I received after I complained to a police department about the way I had been treated during a traffic stop (see Introduction).

Perhaps, then, it is time to closely examine how officers are trained to keep themselves safe out on the street. And rather than completely eliminating traditional street survival courses, it might make sense to start looking on "soft skills" topics such as ethics, cultural diversity, and tactical communication as integral parts of any officer safety regimen. Dr. George Thompson, founder and president of the Verbal Judo Institute, for example, suggests that a strong command of verbal skills is essential to success as a police officer. Emphasizing that cops *should not* take "crap" from people but *should* find ways to deflect it, Thompson says that when it comes to tactical communication, cops should not take abusive words personally. Instead, they should deal with an adversary using only their professional style. He also suggests officers treat others only as they themselves would like to be treated in similar circumstances. H-m-m-m. Sounds like good advice from an "officer safety" point of view. Thompson's suggestion, of course, is identical to the one made by the senior officer in my cultural diversity class several years ago (see Introduction).

Despite its popularity and relevance, ethics training always falls by the wayside with the inevitable budget crunches. Most thoughtful police leaders acknowledge the importance of equipping officers to make informed ethical choices, but when it comes to a budget battle between another round of firearms training and a discussion of character issues in policing . . . well, load up the buses, we're all heading out to the shooting range. This is an unfortunate reality because it places two important programs in competition with one another when, in fact, they both serve to make officers safer out on the street. Let's face it: If I am being placed under arrest by an officer with a reputation for treating prisoners respectfully, not planting evidence, not testifying falsely, and not brutalizing people in her care—in short, treating people *ethically*—the officer will be safer than an officer with a reputation for doing the opposite.

MILITARIZATION OF POLICE

As agencies increasingly emphasize street survival training programs, concerns emerge about what some see as increased militarization by local police. According to Dr. Gary Sykes, writing in *Ethics Roll Call* (summer 2000), the resolution of the Elian Gonzalez case in Miami, Florida, in early 2000 is a good example. Although the mission was successful from a tactical point of view and the boy was retrieved without injury or a shot being fired, many observers were left feeling very uneasy. Part of the reason may have been the widely seen image of the federal officer dressed in combat attire holding an automatic weapon, a photo that provoked enormous political fallout and outspoken disapproval from citizens both inside and outside the Miami community.

Special Weapons and Tactics (SWAT) teams and Mobile Response Teams (MRTs) will continue to perform an important mission in civilian law enforcement, but more and more frequently these types of units are being used for execution of warrants, crowd control, and traffic checkpoints. It is understood that the careful application of force is often necessary to meet the objectives of law

enforcement, but the symbols police agencies use to define themselves and their mission are important. As Dr. Sykes points out,
organizations put their money where their values are, and lots of
money is being invested in militarizing the police.

The concern about officer safety is not a phenomenon that
suddenly came to prominence at the end of the twentieth century.
In his classic police novel *The New Centurions*, Joseph Wambaugh
(1970) describes a lesson taught in a defensive tactics training
class in the Los Angeles Police Academy. An exhausted class of
rookie officers is sprawled around an instructor who has just finished running them to the point of collapse one more time. As the
recruits lie on the ground trying to catch their collective breath,
the instructor shares a profound view of police work that every cop
knows but that many citizens fail to understand:

> Now every one of you guys is going to run into [physical
> resistance] lots of times. Maybe your man is going to
> decide you aren't going to handcuff him. Or maybe he'll
> even fight back. . . . What I'm trying to do is tell you that
> these fights out on the street are just endurance contests.
> The guy who can endure usually wins. That's why I'm
> running your asses off. When you leave here you'll have
> endurance. Now, if I can teach you an armlock and that
> choke hold, maybe that will be enough. You all saw what
> the choke can do. The trouble is getting the choke on the
> guy when he's struggling and fighting back. I can't teach
> you self-defense in thirteen weeks.
>
> All that Hollywood crap is just that—crap. You try
> throwing that haymaker at somebody's chin and you'll
> probably hit the top of his head and break your hand.
> Never use your fists. If someone uses his fists you use your
> stick and try to break a wrist or knee like we teach you. If
> he uses a knife you use a gun and cancel his ticket then
> and there. But if you find yourself without a stick and the
> situation doesn't permit deadly force, well then you better
> be able to out-endure the son of a bitch. That's why you see
> those newspaper pictures of six cops subduing one guy.
> Any guy or even any woman can wear out several police-
> men just by resisting. It's goddamn hard to take a man
> who doesn't want to be taken. But try explaining it to the
> jury or the neighbors who read in the papers how an

arrestee was hurt by two or three cops twice his size. They'll want to know why you resorted to beating the guy's head in. Why didn't you just put a fancy judo hold on him and flip him on his ass. In the movies it's nothing.

For a citizen, understanding the officer safety mind-set of the police can be crucial. For example, when an officer stops your vehicle and orders you to stay in your car and to keep your hands in sight, the message may be delivered in an abrupt and forceful manner, but don't take it personally. If you step too close to an officer and he asks you to move back, it probably has nothing to do with your personal hygiene. If you are being interviewed on the street and the officer orders you to take your hands out of your pockets, don't argue; just do it. In each of these cases, the officer is simply trying to ensure his personal safety.

Over the past ten years or so, several members of the Federal Bureau of Investigation (FBI) have conducted extensive research into the circumstances surrounding events in which police officers are killed or assaulted. Their report (*FBI Law Enforcement Bulletin*, July 2000), which includes interviews with a number of men and women serving time for attacks against police, found that criminals pay very close attention to the behaviors of officers prior to assaulting them. According to the findings of the FBI researchers, most victim officers had similar characteristics:

- They are friendly, laid-back, and easygoing.
- They are well liked by the community and department.
- They are hardworking.
- They desire to look for good in others.
- They tend to use less force than other officers felt they would use in similar circumstances.
- They perceive themselves as more public relations and service oriented than law enforcement directed.
- They tend to not follow all the rules, especially in making arrests, confronting prisoners, enforcing traffic laws, and waiting for backup (when available).
- They sense that they could "read" others and situations and have the tendency to drop their guard as a result.

When you have an official interaction with an officer, it is important to remember that even though you know yourself to be a wholly mild-mannered, cooperative, and nonconfrontational adult, the police officer has not yet learned that. She has just stopped you for running a red light. And while you thought it was yellow just before you glanced at your cell phone to call the office, the officer is still in the process of determining whether your brown 1997 Oldsmobile might not be the brown 1997 Buick seen leaving a bank holdup in an adjoining community ten minutes ago. As a consequence, you may be thinking that the police officer is behaving in a strangely rigid and unfriendly manner. At the same time, the officer is thinking, *I ... am ... going ... home ... to ... my ... family ... at ... the ... end ... of ... my ... shift.*

DISCUSSION QUESTIONS

1. Will training in topics like ethics and cultural diversity help to make police officers safer as they go about their duties? Why or why not?
2. Why is it so difficult for some police officers to "turn off the radar" when they leave work and go home to their families?
3. Is the move toward increased militarization of the police compatible with the growing emphasis on community policing?
4. What are the personal and professional characteristics of a professional, customer-oriented—*and safe*—police officer?

chapter *5*

THE POLICE MISSION GONE AWRY

To the Citizen: Before reading this chapter, think of some high-profile scandals that have affected law enforcement in recent years. Even if they have not touched you or occurred in your community, have they had an impact on how you feel about the police? Has your level of trust in law enforcement been affected? As a citizen, you have given the police considerable power and authority. Do they use that power and authority appropriately?

To the Police Officer: As you read this chapter, consider some of the high-profile scandals that have affected the law enforcement community in the 1990s and into the new century. How many of them have resulted from a misuse of police power and authority? Do bad things sometimes happen in the pursuit of doing good? Do citizens ever have a point when they complain about being singled out by the police? If citizens lack trust in the police, does your job become easier or harder?

Police officers have a right to stop you. As a matter of fact, in many cases, they have an obligation to do so. When we hire police officers, we give them extraordinary power and authority. Yes, we insist that they take an oath as part of the process, but we as citizens give up a considerable portion of our personal rights and liberties in order that our streets and persons remain safe. In return, of course, we agree to vote, pay taxes, serve on a jury if summoned, and go to war if drafted. But for the most part, we'd like the traffic to move smoothly, we'd like the crowd at the ball game to remain orderly, and we'd like to be able to take the dog for a walk at night without fear of being robbed or assaulted. We all want to be safe and secure, but we would rather not have to interact any more than necessary with the people we hire to ensure those conditions for us.

And the reason is simple: When citizens find themselves interacting with the police, the circumstances that brought them together are generally stressful and often unhappy. And police officers understand this. For example, somewhere in the city next Saturday night, there will be a group of people sitting around having a good time, maybe eating pizza and maybe drinking a few beers. Cops know that in the midst of this relaxed and congenial gathering, these words will *never* be spoken: "Hey, we're having such a good time. Let's invite the police over to join us!" Police officers know that the only time they will be summoned to that location is when trouble breaks out and someone has to bring order out of chaos.

There is a long-standing quasi-serious rivalry between police officers and firefighters, with each convinced the other is overpaid and underworked. Recently, an officer from a midsized city lamented that in a satisfaction survey rating various city services, citizens in his community had ranked the fire department about four points higher than the police. The solution to help level the playing field, the officer suggested, was to "have the firefighters start writing tickets." He was kidding, of course, but the fact is that when firefighters arrive on a scene, citizens perceive them as being there to help. When the police show up, the nature of their job is such that some citizens don't necessarily see them as being particularly helpful.

For law enforcement officers to be able to adequately do their jobs, we citizens give them considerable power, authority, and even leeway. For example, under certain circumstances, we allow them to stop us when we are walking or driving; when conditions warrant, we permit ourselves to be "patted down" for their protection; and, occasionally, we allow them to employ extreme methods to apprehend criminals and keep us safe. As we citizens willingly set aside some of our rights and grant authority to the police, though, citizens and police alike must be clear about the source of police power: It flows directly from the very citizens who are being policed. As such, we have a legitimate right to expect open and honest accountability for the manner in which law enforcement power and authority are being utilized.

In the noble quest to do good, police officers sometimes misuse their authority. Fortunately, it doesn't happen very often; unfortunately, when it does happen, it is extremely hard to detect. After all, the criminal justice system gives considerable weight to the sworn testimony of an officer, so a lie under oath can pass unnoticed except for the protest of the accused. For example, an officer may believe that sending a particularly troublesome gang member to prison as quickly as possible is a good thing for the community, and many residents would likely agree with her. But in bringing about this "good" result, the officer may decide to plant evidence on the gang member and then testify falsely against him: a "good" end brought about by "bad" means. The gang member may complain or even raise an objection at trial, but who is going to listen to someone like him?

In carrying out the difficult, dangerous, and righteous work of policing, the words of Friedrich Nietzsche should provide a strong and thoughtful message of caution:

> Those who fight the monster need to take care that it does not turn them into monsters.

In the discussion to follow, think carefully about the manner in which police officers use the extraordinary power at their disposal. At the same time, consider how many, and which, of your own rights you—police officer and citizen alike—would be willing to limit or even give up in the name of keeping our communities as crime-free as possible.

STOPPING YOU IN A CAR

Do you have a taillight out on your vehicle? The police can stop you. Is your license plate even partly obscured? You can be pulled over. Are you speeding or weaving from lane to lane? You could easily be the subject of a traffic stop. Do you look like you "don't belong in the neighborhood"? A police officer can pull your vehicle over, but, based solely on your "not fitting the area," he shouldn't.

The courts have repeatedly held that police officers need some verifiable reason to stop a vehicle, but a cop with even a rudimentary knowledge of the vehicle and traffic laws knows there are countless potential (and obscure) violations that can be used to pull you over. Have you driven onto the shoulder of the road in order to pass a vehicle in front of you making a left turn? Are you driving too fast or too slow? Is your rearview mirror obscured? How dark is that window tint? Is your child properly secured? Each of these minor but legitimate violations could give an officer sufficient grounds to stop your vehicle.

Sometimes obscure traffic laws are in place for specific roads and bridges, and even the most well-informed citizen would be hard-pressed to know them. In New York State, for example, certain parkways under the jurisdiction of the East Hudson Parkway Authority (EHPA) had, for many years, a voluminous set of traffic rules applicable only to motorists on these specific roads. Ignorance of the law, of course, is never a valid defense, so a motorist who happened to stop along the parkway to pick some flowers or take a picture could be in big trouble (stopping along the road for these purposes was a violation). And heaven forbid someone should operate a commercial vehicle on these specific roads or be caught driving a car with lettering on the side larger than the prescribed dimensions. For many police officers, the most delicious aspect of having such rules was not that they *had* to be enforced but rather that they *could* be enforced.

Perhaps an example would be helpful. One summer afternoon, a police officer patrolling the Taconic State Parkway in New York State stopped a van-like vehicle with what looked like a rack suitable for carrying ladders or other construction tools on the top. And although no materials were being carried and no company logos or advertising was displayed on the van, in the officer's mind, the rack made the van commercial and therefore prohibited vehicle. When the officer approached the driver, he asked, "What is that up on the top of your van?" The motorist (armed with marginal knowledge of the EHPA rules and regulations himself) said to the officer in tones dripping with sarcasm, "Let's just say those are ski racks." (Ski racks were permitted on vehicles on this road.) The officer, without missing a beat in the conversation, replied, "Well, let's just say your 'ski racks' are protruding more than nine inches from the top of your van" (a violation). In other words, the driver's valiant attempt at using an obscure rule in his defense had been trumped by the officer's knowledge of an even more obscure rule.

As mentioned earlier, police officers need a reason for stopping your vehicle. Sometimes (and, thankfully, not very often), these reasons are fabricated. The NBC television program *Dateline* investigated traffic stops along Interstate 10 in Louisiana in 1996 and found that officers would sometimes stop a car and accuse the driver of speeding or swerving out of a driving lane, all despite video evidence that no such violation had occurred. In California in 1989 an ABC television investigation into allegations of racial profiling revealed that Long Beach police stopped a vehicle and accused the driver of swerving across the centerline of the roadway, even though video taken by a following vehicle showed no such violation to have occurred.

Beyond the videotaped examples of police lying about reasons for traffic stops, a great deal of anecdotal evidence feeds suspicions that citizens are sometimes being stopped without just cause. One need only listen to reputable people of goodwill who cite repeated examples of being pulled over for any number of reasons, both legitimate and illegitimate. Is it because of the color of the motorist's skin? Could it be due to some mandate that the flow of drugs along the highways be stopped at all costs? Might these traffic stops derive from some organizational emphasis on arrests and seizures of contraband as the means to get promoted? Or is it some combination of these factors?

The issue of traffic stops based on inappropriate means has a contemporary name—profiling, or driving while black (DWB). (This issue is discussed further later in this chapter.) But from time to time, reports of outrageous misuse of police authority surface for other reasons as well. Rare though they may be, these outrageous acts of misbehavior make the task of reinforcing the public trust even tougher.

STOPPING YOU ON THE STREET

In much the same fashion as you can be stopped while operating a motor vehicle, police officers have the authority to detain you and, in many cases, ask you for identification and even "pat you down." But there are some basic differences between the traffic stop and the pedestrian stop, and many of them have to do with the all-important issue of officer safety. In a traffic stop situation, after all, there is little likelihood of any contact between officer and citizen unless it is initiated by the officer. On the street, though, contacts can be brought about through a variety of means.

Generally speaking, police officers have a right to stop citizens who are walking along the street and who may have given the officers reason to believe they may be engaged in some form of misbehavior. In fact, these are the very conditions under which citizens

ABUSING AUTHORITY AND GETTING AWAY WITH IT

When police officers abuse their authority, that act is often very difficult to detect and prove. Violating citizen rights is serious business, after all, so cops who do it tend to select their victims carefully. They look for people who will likely remain quiet. Two particularly vulnerable groups are those who may be concerned about their own questionable legal status and those fearful of embarrassment.

In recent years, several police agencies across the United States have investigated officers charged with stopping vehicles driven by illegal immigrants and then, rather than citing or arresting the occupants, simply taking money from them. Frankly, a corrupt cop could not ask for a better target. The victim (who is in the United States illegally to begin with) knows that if he reports the theft, it will be his word against that of a police officer, and regardless of the outcome, he will likely be deported.

In early 2001, an East Coast agency was rocked by allegations that an officer stopped a young woman for drunk driving and then, instead of placing her under arrest, permitted her to walk home . . . naked. When the case was reported in the newspaper, a number of other young women contacted the department reporting that they, too, had been treated in a similar fashion by that same cop. They had remained silent because they feared humiliation and embarrassment.

In March 2002, the officer involved in this case was indicted for violating the civil rights of four women he forced to disrobe after pulling them over for traffic violations. He pleaded guilty in April 2003 and currently faces up to five years in jail.

would argue that police have an *obligation* to stop and inquire of a suspicious person; that is, after all, why we employ police officers in the first place. But infringing on someone's freedom of movement is always a complicated issue, and it is important to remember that citizens have a right to walk unmolested in public places. Therefore, when a police officer detains them, that officer must be able to articulate the reasons why the stop was made.

ENTERING YOUR HOME

In any discussion about the right of police to enter your home uninvited, the eloquent and timeless words of William Pitt, earl of Chatham (1708–1788), come to mind. Speaking on the absolute sanctity of each citizen's home, he wrote:

> The poorest man may in his cottage bid defiance to all the force of the Crown. It may be frail; its roof may shake; the wind may blow through it; the storms may enter, the rain may enter—but the King of England cannot enter; all his forces dare not cross the threshold of the ruined tenement!

Even today, Pitt's words ring true, for it is well established that police officers may not generally enter a private residence except with a warrant or some other similar justification. There are certain narrow exceptions (hot pursuit and "no knock" warrants, for example), but, generally speaking, the government may not arbitrarily enter a dwelling. And any time the police rely on exceptions or exigent circumstances to enter a home or conduct a search, they must be able to articulate the precise reasons for their actions.

This is not to say the police cannot get into your domicile if they really want to. In New Westminster, British Columbia (see Chapter 2), the police wanted to enter the residences of several drug suspects, so they invited representatives from the health and fire departments along on their visits. Since officials from these agencies often have considerably more authority than the police to enter buildings (including homes) to look for life-threatening violations, it is not uncommon for law enforcement agencies to use their assistance to gain entry where they might otherwise be unable to tread.

In June 2000, two officers from the St. Paul, Minnesota, Police Department used an innovative ploy in their attempt to gain entry to a suspected drug house: They represented themselves as workers for the U.S. Census Bureau. When the ruse was brought to light, the police chief assured the public that his officers would no longer use this strategy. Needless to say, the chief's statement brought considerable relief to people actually employed by the Census Bureau. Their jobs were already difficult enough without having to fear whether citizens would wonder if they were undercover police officers as they went about their duties.

RACIAL PROFILING

On October 22, 1999, New Jersey State Superior Court Judge Victor Friedman had just finished consolidating cases involving eighteen defendants in Burlington County, who claimed they had been unfairly stopped because of their race. Apparently Judge Friedman had seen and heard quite enough; in carefully chosen words, he said, "Racial profiling, in general, was at one time considered a theory or allegation." He added: "At this point, racial profiling is a fact." He then stunned the courtroom with a sweeping directive that would require analysis of the facts of every traffic stop made anywhere on the New Jersey Turnpike since 1993.

As he spoke, the full extent of his order became clear; the state was, for the first time, being ordered to provide defense attorneys with information on racial profiling by members of the New Jersey State Police that included internal reports, traffic data, arrest reports, and, most significantly, a police officer personnel records. The deputy attorney general representing the state immediately argued that some of the information demanded by the order was privileged and therefore should not be disclosed. In response, Judge Friedman directed that any appeals of his order be specific and well documented, adding "Privilege is not another word for cover-up."

In his order and comments, Judge Friedman went directly to the heart of the racial profiling debate in the United States. The fact of the matter is that in the year 2003, we should not be surprised that many people of color have doubts when they are pulled over by the police. Did I commit a violation? Or was it the color of my skin? Few citizens are unfamiliar with this issue. And much like the alcoholic who says he doesn't have a drinking problem while everyone around him sees his decline and ruin, police officers who say there is no such thing as racial profiling are living in denial.

The Definition, Explanation, and Justification for Profiling

In the cultural diversity arena, discrimination—based on a number of factors—can be either rational or irrational. Making sure that I never be allowed to perform cardiac surgery or that a sightless person not be hired as a baseball umpire, for example, is not only rational discrimination but good common sense as well. To

exclude someone from a position for which she is otherwise qualified based simply on gender or the color of her skin would, obviously, fall into the category of irrational discrimination.

Similarly, there is both rational profiling and irrational profiling. Rational profiling (also known as criminal profiling) is a
legitimate investigative tool in the fight against crime, and sensible police officers use it all the time. It is a method by which
officers, through careful observation of activities and environment, identify suspicious people and, in context, develop a legal
reason to stop them for questioning. Irrational profiling (also
known as racial profiling) refers to those times when a police
officer decides to stop and question someone when the sole
rationale for that intervention is the race of the person being
stopped.

Profiling, then, is a valid and important tool that police officers use to make themselves both effective and safe and is very
different from racial profiling. The Arlington, Virginia, Police
Department's "Statement on Racial Profiling" (1999) reads in part:

> We must understand that proper police tactics can be
> experienced by innocent people as frightening and alien-
> ating. We must recognize that many of the people we stop
> will be released without further action. In this context,
> we believe that how our authority is employed is as
> important as the results of its use.
>
> We know that the act of stopping an unknown sub-
> ject frequently occurs under ambiguous and dangerous
> circumstances. Our commitment to employees requires,
> in our profession, a commitment to officer safety. One of
> the strongest guarantees of officer safety is community
> support and acceptance.
>
> We are the inheritors of a social history that has
> been marked by racial and ethnic discord and distrust.
> Our profession has a duty not to contribute to that dis-
> cord; instead, we must establish relationships based on
> trust with all our communities. (P.E.R.F., "Subject to
> Debate," December 1999, p. 5)

In Ventura, California, the police department has developed
and disseminated an agency philosophy designed to ensure professional traffic stops. It reads:

Proactive traffic enforcement is an effective strategy to protect the public from the devastation caused by drug abuse, street and highway traffic-related death and injury, illegal trafficking in and possession of weapons, and continued freedom of fugitives, and to otherwise promote and maintain an orderly and law-abiding society.

Proactive traffic enforcement must and will continue to be conducted in fullest compliance with the constitutional and statutory safeguards established to preserve the rights of citizens, the prescriptions of case law and the sanctioned policies and practices of law enforcement agencies.

Proactive traffic enforcement that is racially or ethnically based is neither legal, consistent with democratic ideals, values and principles of American policing, nor in any way a legitimate and defensible public protection strategy. It is not, cannot, and will not be tolerated by this Department. (Ventura, California, Policy Manual Sec. 102.13.2)

The History and Evolution of Racial Profiling

If it is necessary to pick a specific time as the beginning of the racial profiling discussion, 1982 is probably appropriate. That year, the federal government undertook a highly intensive air and sea operation in the South Florida region to combat the smuggling of drugs into the United States. Other agencies, including the Florida Highway Patrol, became involved in the effort, and in 1985 the Florida Department of Highway Safety and Motor Vehicles issued a set of guidelines to help law enforcement personnel identify potential drug smugglers along the highways. These guidelines, called "Common Characteristics of Drug Couriers," suggested that police officers be watchful for a number of indicators, including the following:

- People driving rental cars
- Drivers who scrupulously obey traffic laws
- Drivers wearing "lots of gold"
- Drivers who do not "fit" the vehicle
- Ethnic groups associated with the drug trade

The Police Mission Gone Awry

Very quickly, a number of police officers from jurisdictions across the United States became quite adept at using such indicators to join the war on drugs, and the results were phenomenal. Large quantities of illegal drugs and money were seized, and many arrests were made. As a result, training programs sprang up to teach even more officers how to use indicators to identify potential drug couriers, lawfully stop them, and then develop sufficient cause or willing consent for a vehicle search. Some programs even recommended particular types of tools officers should carry to help open hidden compartments where drugs were often carried and showed where such storage areas could be found on different makes and models of vehicles.

In the mid-1980s, the Drug Courier program was so wildly successful that the U.S. Drug Enforcement Administration, through an effort known as Operation Pipeline, became actively involved in conducting and underwriting highway drug interdiction training programs for law enforcement agencies across the United States.

At about the same time (middle to late 1980s), most major cities in the United States were overrun by a crack epidemic. In response, many big-city police departments initiated major efforts to deal with street-level drug dealing: New York City launched Operation Pressure Point, Chicago had Operation Invincible, and Los Angeles rolled out Operation Hammer. The announced target of their efforts (street-level drug trade), of course, is generally confined to inner-city neighborhoods populated by people of color and is relatively open and therefore easy to deal with. Not surprisingly, therefore, minorities tended to be disproportionately represented among those arrested.

The goal of the antidrug efforts in big cities during this period was to make as many arrests as possible, and, to that end, the programs succeeded admirably. Between 1981 and 1988, national arrests for drug possession almost doubled, rising from 400,000 to 762,718. Likewise, arrests for drug sale and manufacture jumped at about the same rate, increasing from 150,000 to 287,858. But, as pointed out, with enforcement efforts targeted at the inner city, most of those taken into custody were either black or Hispanic, feeding the misperception that drug use and manufacture are largely the province of people from these racial or ethnic groups. In reality, U.S. Department of Justice data reveal that 80 percent of U.S. cocaine users are middle-class, white suburbanites (American

Civil Liberties Union, "Racial Profiling on Our Nation's Highways," p. 4).

In the late 1990s, as the racial profiling debate was being raised across the United States, the New Jersey State Police (NJSP) was particularly hard hit by allegations that officers routinely stopped and searched motorists for no reason other than race. Agency leaders repeatedly denied such charges, and political leaders generally stood solidly behind them—at least until early 1996. In March of that year, a state superior court judge in Gloucester County, New Jersey, challenged the solid denials of the NJSP when he dismissed charges against seventeen black defendants, ruling that they had been stopped because of their race.

Under mounting pressure, the New Jersey attorney general undertook a study of traffic stops made by members of the NJSP between 1997 and 1999 and found some interesting patterns. For example, during the study period, the racial makeup of motorists stopped by New Jersey troopers was 59.4 percent white and 27 percent black. During this same period, statistics revealed that 77.2 percent of the searches conducted were of black or Hispanic motorists. The numbers were revealing, and on April 20, 1999, the attorney general issued a report in which he acknowledged "subtle factors of a police culture . . . [with] unclear guidelines . . . [and a] misguided impression that they may use race as a factor" (Peterson, *New York Times*, April 21, 1999, p. 4).

For at least one New Jersey trooper, there was very little confusion about the guidelines he was to follow; on CBS's *60 Minutes* (October 20, 1999), Trooper Greg Sanders said, "Racial profiling is trained. It's taught at the academy and it's taught at in-service training. It was condoned. It was rewarded. And if you didn't participate in it, you were punished for it." In Peterson's interview for the *New York Times* on April 21, 1999, New Jersey Governor Christine Todd Whitman pointed out that although no official policy permitting racial profiling existed, in her view management styles, coaching of state troopers by superiors, and a system that rewarded both aggressive ticket writing and drug seizures had combined to create an atmosphere that went beyond simple racism to "a problem that is more complex and subtle than we first realized" (*New York Times*, April 21, 1999, p. 1).

Incidentally, the New Jersey attorney general used incomplete data when he released those figures in his April 1999 report showing 77.2 percent of searches were of black and Hispanic motorists. He did not know the data were incomplete at the time; only on July 26, 2000, did a three-year-old internal NJSP memorandum written by a sergeant and addressed to the then-superintendent come to light. In it, the sergeant detailed a NJSP survey of 160 searches conducted by troopers at the Moorestown barracks from April to December 1994 and again from July to December 1996. According to the memo, minority drivers accounted for 89 percent of those searched. "At this point we are in a very bad spot," related the sergeant. "The Justice Department has a very good understanding of how we operate and what type of numbers they can get their hands on to prove their position."

Also on the East Coast, the head of the Maryland State Police (MSP), in an interview with the *New York Times* published on June 5, 1998, vigorously defended his organization against allegations of racial profiling. "Let me make this crystal clear," he said. "The Maryland state police has not ever, does not ever and will not ever condone the use of race-based profiling. It's against the law, and it will not be tolerated" (American Civil Liberties Union, "Racial Profiling on Our Nation's Highways," p. 5). And the superintendent should know what he's talking about because his agency has been involved in several race profiling lawsuits over the years. As a result of a 1993 lawsuit (*Wilkins* v. *Maryland State Police*), for example, the MSP was required to keep computer records of all searches of motorists in order to permit monitoring for patterns of discrimination. In 1996 the American Civil Liberties Union of Maryland, using the data the MSP collected, asked the court to hold the Maryland State Police in contempt.

A look at the data collected by the Maryland State Police is instructive. For example, between January 1995 and September 1996, the agency reported searching 823 drivers on Interstate 95 north of Baltimore; 661 (80.3 percent) were black, Hispanic, or other racial minorities. Most of these searches (85.4 percent) were conducted by thirteen troopers. Table 5.1 shows statistics for some of the troopers who conducted ten or more searches along that highway during the study period.

Remember, these numbers were maintained by the Maryland State Police *while they knew they were under scrutiny*. When these

TABLE 5.1 Searches by Maryland State Police (1/95–9/96)

	TOTAL SEARCHED	MINORITIES SEARCHED	PERCENT BLACKS SEARCHED	PERCENT MINORITIES SEARCHED
Trooper A	68	58	75.0	85.3
Trooper B	12	12	100.0	100.0
Trooper C	30	27	76.7	90.0
Trooper D	65	55	81.5	84.6
Trooper E	37	11	21.6	39.7
Trooper F	150	131	83.3	87.3
Trooper G	70	59	81.4	84.3
Trooper H	32	26	59.4	81.3
Trooper I	40	39	97.5	97.5

types of issues are raised for discussion in a training program with in-service officers, two questions commonly arise:

1. *What is the race of the officer conducting the search?* This is an interesting question that somehow seems to infer that a motorist stopped because of race might be less bothered or humiliated if the officer who has pulled him or her over is also a member of a minority group.
2. *Are these searches successful?* This is an excellent question that speaks directly to the ends-means argument concerning law enforcement tactics. Actually, highway drug interdiction efforts are typically wildly successful in terms of drugs, contraband, and money recovered and arrests made. The problem is, of course, that many innocent people get caught in the net that is thrown out to catch wrongdoers.

One agency that has been particularly successful at using traffic stops to make drug arrests and seize money and contraband has been the Volusia County, Florida, Sheriff's Department Drug Squad. The *Orlando Sentinel*, in August 1992, obtained 148 hours of in-car videotapes, which revealed that some 75 percent of all motorists stopped were black or Hispanic and only 9 out of 1,084 stops resulted in traffic tickets being issued. The focus of the stops, it seems, was a search for cash, with thousands of dollars seized from motorists who were never charged with an offense.

In Orange County, Florida, the Sheriff's Drug Squad made 3,800 traffic stops and conducted 500 searches between January 1996 and April 1997. According to the *Orlando Sentinel* (June 1997), blacks accounted for 16.3 percent of those stopped but were searched 39.6 percent of the time. White drivers were searched 6.2 percent of the time. Overall, black motorists made up more than 50 percent of the total searches and more than 70 percent of searches conducted using canine units.

There can be no doubt that the issue of profile police stops continues to resonate in the public consciousness, as evidenced by its increasingly frequent exploration in the world of comedy. After all, professional comedians often provide a wonderfully precise and edgy snapshot of current events and the world as it really is. For example, when professional golfer Tiger Woods identified himself several years ago as Cablinasian (a mixture of Caucasian, black, Asian, and Indian), one African American comic pointed out, "If Tiger thinks he's a 'Cablinasian,' wait until the police pull him over because he's black."

But some people continue to maintain there is no such thing as racial profiling. As you might imagine, there is usually considerable tension when a group of police officers come together to discuss the issue of racial profiling. Cops see themselves as being under enormous scrutiny and pressure on this issue, and, as a consequence, there is often a great deal of heated debate, rationalization, and denial that the problem even exists. From time to time, though, something happens in the room that instantly turns down the volume of this frequently rancorous discussion and moves it in a dramatically different (and more enlightening) direction. This powerful (and unpredictable) shift occurs when an African American or Latino officer who happens to be in the group decides—on his or her own—to speak up on the issue.

When a course facilitator who happens to be white leads a discussion of racial profiling, it is easy for participants to dismiss the facilitator as uninformed about the real world of policing out on the street. But when a racial minority police officer begins sharing personal experiences of being pulled over without having committed a violation, the room becomes quiet. When a black officer describes how it feels to be stopped without cause by another police officer, his words have considerable impact. When a Latino sergeant talks about the number of times she was pulled over without justification while driving an older car from Texas to deliver it to her brother in Michigan, other officers in the room listen uncomfortably. When police officers are willing to speak up and identify themselves as being among the victims of racial profiling, others in the room are able to put a familiar face on the issue. When a colleague describes the hurt and indignity suffered at the hands of other members of the profession, the issue comes to life in vivid and unforgettable fashion.

THE RAMPART SCANDAL IN THE LOS ANGELES POLICE DEPARTMENT

As the details of the investigation of the Rampart Division of the Los Angeles Police Department (LAPD) continued to unfold through 1999 and into 2000, new and ever more breathtaking accusations of police misbehavior seemed to surface almost daily. One of the most startling outrages involved the Community Resources Against Street Hoodlums (CRASH) unit; a sizable number of criminal convictions have been overturned because of a pattern of lying by CRASH police officers. In other words, police officers did a bad thing (lied under oath) in order to do a good thing (rid the neighborhoods of gang members). Note carefully, by the way, that these are *convictions* that have been overturned; this is a very different and far more serious matter than an arrest a prosecutor chose not to take to trial or a court case that resulted in an acquittal. What this means is that defendants have in many cases been sent to prison unjustly. It also means the city of Los Angeles expects to pay handsomely to compensate them.

The full monetary cost of the Rampart scandal will not be known for many years, but there is no doubt it will be enormous. According to an editorial in the *Los Angeles Times* ("Rampart's Rising Costs," May 12, 2000), the Los Angeles City Council budgeted $41 million for liability costs, investigation, and police reforms in the coming year. This figure, by the way, was in addition to the city's $300 million tobacco settlement windfall, which had already been redirected into a fund to (hopefully) cover the costs of the lawsuits anticipated as a result of Rampart. Stop for a moment and read that again: That is *$300 million* that could have gone for parks, swimming pools, and other infrastructure repairs or city services to make Los Angeles a better and more livable city. Instead, it is being set aside to pay claims expected from victims of law enforcement misbehavior.

The financial pain of the Rampart scandal is being felt in Los Angeles County as well. In May 2000 the estimated costs to the county district attorney and public defender offices for finding and working on tainted Los Angeles Police Department cases stood at $11.4 million, and the number continued to rise. This figure, by the way, amounted to 25 percent of every new dollar of revenue expected by the county in the new fiscal year. And as with the city of Los Angeles, this means commensurately less can be spent on other vital county services.

Although the costs in terms of money will be substantial, at the end of the day, the greatest harm to the LAPD will likely be far more personal. For many years to come, the good, upstanding, and hardworking officers who overwhelmingly populate the LAPD will be viewed with suspicion because of the evil deeds of a very few of their corrupt colleagues. And for many citizens, trust in the Los Angeles police was already very badly shaken as a result of the O. J. Simpson debacle. As one resident said after that trial:

> I don't even put quarters in parking meters anymore. After Fuhrman, police in this town couldn't get a conviction for a parking ticket.

THE NEW YORK CITY POLICE STREET CRIME UNIT

As one of the "kings of late-night television," David Letterman is known for making outrageous remarks about life in New York City. And even though people who live there might laugh at his jokes, they know there is an edgy element of truth to many of his observations. For example, when he notes that "New York now leads the world's great cities in the number of people around whom you shouldn't make a sudden move," New Yorkers chuckle but nod knowingly. And to many city residents, there was more fact than humor in his boast to the rest of the world that "When civilization falls apart, remember, we were way ahead of you" (Letterman, 1984).

Former New York City Mayor Rudy Giuliani, however, never found such comments amusing. In the mid-1990s Giuliani, along with Police Commissioner Howard Safir, launched a citywide initiative to turn New York into a safe, clean visitor- and resident-friendly place. Emphasizing enforcement of quality-of-life issues, the now-defunct New York City Police Department (NYPD) Street

Crime Unit (SCU) found itself on the front lines of that effort. (The SCU was disbanded in April 2002.) A small (about 2 percent of the total strength of the NYPD) and elite unit, the SCU was tasked with stopping crime before it happened. As a result, members of the SCU were engaged in a great deal of face-to-face, direct, hands-on, confrontational interactions with citizens. They were also adept at developing probable cause very quickly and skilled in the legitimacy and propriety of pat-downs, stop-and-frisk, stops based on a reasonable and articulable suspicion of criminal activity, and other types of citizen interventions. And, given the small size of the unit, the SCU was extraordinarily productive, making approximately 40 percent of the illegal firearms arrests in New York City.

Needless to say, the SCU had a history of very impressive work. The unit was so impressive, in fact, that at an awards ceremony, Commissioner Howard Safir suggested that if there were a way to "bottle the enthusiasm of that unit," he would do so and have all the other members of the department "take a drink." When he then proposed that the size of the SCU be dramatically increased, commanders of the unit objected. Pointing out the complex and stressful nature of street crime work, they predicted significant difficulty in training and supervising large numbers of new members in the nuances of search and seizure. Not to be deterred, Safir tripled the number of personnel assigned to SCU.

Operationally, Street Crime Unit members were supposed to keep a running count of the number of citizens they stopped and interacted with, and by their own calculations, in 1998 and 1999 they stopped approximately 45,000 individuals. During that same period and from the ranks of those reported stopped, they arrested almost 9,000. Doing the math, this means approximately 36,000 citizens were stopped by members of the SCU in some official fashion and at the end of the interaction were allowed to go on their way. As an aside, some former members of the SCU say these numbers were artificially low, maintaining that some officers filled out the required forms only about one out of ten times.

Since the Street Crime Unit did much of its work in inner-city neighborhoods, a significant number of those 45,000 or so citizens with whom they interacted in 1998 and 1999 were likely people of color. That being the case, it is important to note that prior to the unit being reconstituted after the Amadou Diallo shooting in February 1999, the makeup of the unit was about 10 percent racial minority, while the overall NYPD was approximately 30 percent racial minority.

Given the intensity and nature of the work its members were required to do, there are some other facts about the SCU that may have affected how group members went about their tasks and the way citizens perceived their job performance. First of all, the motto of the Street Crime Unit was "We Own the Night." It appears to have been at least quasi-official, because it could be glimpsed on a banner during press conferences where SCU members displayed weapons they took off the street. In addition, there is evidence that some members of the Street Crime Unit wore T-shirts bearing the following quote from Ernest Hemingway:

> Certainly there is no hunting like the hunting of man and those who have hunted armed men long enough and liked it, never really care for anything else thereafter.

Shortcomings of police management will be addressed more fully in Chapter 6, but given the way the SCU appeared to see itself and its mission in 1998 and 1999, there is an important supervisory question begging an answer: Where were the bosses? Let's face it: When a police unit feels empowered to broadcast the fact that it *owns* the night and then appears to underline that philosophy with a T-shirt that glorifies the *hunting* of men, something is terribly amiss. Police officers are not members of the military, after all; they represent *civilian* law enforcement. As such, their supervisors must be prepared to step in when necessary to bring things back into focus. The point here, of course, is not about a unit motto or a T-shirt slogan. The heart of this matter, really, is what these things symbolize and what they broadcast to others about the way police officers see themselves, their duties, and the citizens they are sworn to serve.

The Street Crime Unit was at the center of the incident in February 1999 in which Amadou Diallo, an African immigrant, was shot and killed in the vestibule of his home by four members of the SCU. In the process of approaching Diallo to interview him (he fit the general description of a rapist who was being sought in the area), the officers observed him make a movement toward his pocket, a gesture they interpreted as potentially threatening. When he withdrew an object they thought might be a handgun, they fired forty-one rounds at him, striking him a total of nineteen times. It turns out that the object he had taken from his pocket was his wallet.

The officers involved in the Diallo incident were acquitted of criminal charges in early 2000, and almost one year later, the federal government decided against charging them with civil rights violations. In the spring of 2001, the NYPD determined that deficient training was to blame for this horrific event and said the officers would not be disciplined for their actions. The legal exposure for the four officers has not ended, however, for a separate trial for damages in civil court is yet to be heard. But this incident (and others like it) have given voice to a number of inner-city residents (and others) who question the legitimacy of a system that seems to authorize police to skirt individual civil liberties in the quest for "safe streets" and "quality of life." In other words, although citizens want to be able to live in a safe neighborhood, they don't want to have to pay such an exorbitant price in terms of human lives and erosion of rights to do so.

THE POWER OF SYMBOLS

Fact: A nationally prominent police defensive tactics trainer who travels around the United States teaching officers how to keep themselves safe in a variety of situations always concludes his classes in exactly the same way. After he has given students their course certificates, he hands them each a pin bearing the simple message: "We're the biggest street gang in America. We're the police."

Question: Would any police officer want to get on the witness stand and explain why he chooses to describe himself as a member of a street gang? Street gangs are generally understood to be composed of violent, antisocial people typically engaged in some form of criminal behavior. Why would law enforcement officers suggest they see themselves that way?

Fact: A police chief in the Southwest has a Special Weapons and Tactics (SWAT) team in his agency. He recently learned that the members of the unit wear a T-shirt they designed. On the front of the T-shirt are the words "Happiness is . . ."; on the back of the T-shirt it says "A Green Light." (The phrase *green light*, in this context, usually means a SWAT team member has received authorization to use deadly physical force.)

Question: Why would SWAT team members want to send such a message? No police officer actively seeks opportunities to use deadly force, so such a slogan makes light of the most onerous decision a SWAT officer could ever face. When an officer is forced to take a human life, she must later appear before a grand jury to explain her actions. If the officer is known to have worn a T-shirt with a flippant message about the use of deadly force, will it be easier or harder for her to explain what she did?

Fact: A police academy physical fitness instructor leading a class of recruit police officers on a morning run in 1999 noticed that they had all begun wearing a T-shirt as a means of promoting group cohesion. The class T-shirt displayed the image of one of the characters from the *South Park* television show, along with the words "Respect My Authority."

Question: As the recruits go on their morning run in the neighborhoods around the police academy—the neighborhoods they will be policing once they graduate—are they giving any thought to the message being sent by their T-shirt slogan? What's with this apparent emphasis on authority so early in a career? And while police officers are, of course, deserving of respect, wouldn't it be a good idea for academy recruits to think of respect as something they owe the public as well?

Fact: The Community Resources Against Street Hoodlums unit in the Rampart Division of the Los Angeles Police Department was at the center of a scandal that overwhelmed that organization. Over the door to its unit hung a sign with the motto "We Intimidate Those Who Intimidate Others."

Question: Was this really the mission of the police officers in that unit? To intimidate? Some would say their job was to protect life and property, detect and arrest criminals, provide evidence and testimony in court, and send wrongdoers (when deserved) to jail. The fundamental issue here is the lack of courage and foresight by CRASH supervisors, who should have recognized the problem of a group of officers who saw themselves as "avenging angels" and thereafter brought them back under control.

Again, the point of this discussion is less about a particular slogan or design on a shirt or a pin and more about what these things symbolize to others. As a retired police officer, I understand the importance of creating group solidarity in a team of officers who go out every day and do a dangerous and difficult job, and edgy, cynical statements appearing on shirts, banners, or squad room walls tend to demonstrate, more than anything else, the gallows humor so common in policing. The problem is that sometimes citizens don't get the joke. Instead of laughing, some see these symbols as another manifestation of the tension that already exists between them and the cops on the street. And as trust in law enforcement declines, the job of the police officer becomes even more difficult.

Since 1993 the crime rate has plummeted 55 percent in New York City, and the number of homicides has dropped a startling 65 percent. Yet in spite of these dramatic figures, many city residents feel alienated by their police department. In a poll commissioned by the New York City Council and reported in the *New York Times* (Chivers, September 15, 2000), 1,500 city residents were interviewed between July 31 and August 7, 2000; 61 percent of all New Yorkers said they thought the NYPD had done a good or excellent job. On the other hand, 42 percent of blacks and 36 percent of Hispanics reported feeling "fearful" or "somewhat concerned" when seeing a police officer walk toward them. In addition, 51 percent of white residents said they believed the department engaged in racial profiling, compared with 79 percent of blacks and 66 percent of Hispanics. Finally, an overwhelming majority of all New Yorkers think the NYPD should be overseen by an independent group.

In a Gallup poll conducted in June 2000, public confidence in criminal justice was ranked far below institutions such as banking, the medical system, public schools, television news, newspapers, the military, and the presidency. In fact, this poll (gallup.com/poll/surveys/2000/topline000622/q7.asp) found the criminal justice system to have received the third-lowest level of public confidence among the seventeen institutions listed, with only big business and health maintenance organizations ranked lower. A similar Gallup poll conducted in 1998 reported significant racial division of opinion on faith in the criminal justice system, with almost twice as many whites (61 percent) reporting confidence in the police as blacks (34 percent).

Since September 11, 2001, the nature of police officer-citizen relations has been the subject of robust discussion and close examination. What effects, after all, did the events that horrible day have on the way cops and civilians tend to see one another? In one law enforcement supervision class in June 2002, as a matter of fact, a sergeant demanded to know whether the first edition of this book (*When Cultures Clash*) had been written prior to the World Trade Center disaster, pointing out that—in his view—citizens now tended to see police officers in a far more positive light than before that awful event. As that sergeant rightly pointed out, the sacrifices made by police, fire, and rescue workers at the World Trade Center catastrophe call for quiet reverence and should hold a special place in the hearts of every American. Few have put it as well as Peggy Noonan in her poignant comments in the *Wall Street Journal* (June 11, 2003):

> The men and women working in the towers were there that morning, and died. The firemen and rescue workers—they weren't there, they went there. They didn't run from the fire, they ran into the fire. They didn't run down the staircase, they ran up the staircase. They didn't lose their lives, they gave them.

Doubtless, most would agree that the countless acts of valor and heroism by police, fire, and rescue workers on 9/11 ought to evoke a new and deeper appreciation for what it means to labor in those professions. But it is important to ask whether those feelings of warmth, support, and understanding are permanent or transitory. In her book titled *Are Cops Racist?* Heather MacDonald interviewed one NYPD officer who harbored little doubt about how long the "honeymoon" lasted. Right after 9/11, he told her bluntly, the way people referred to him went from [Insult] to Mister. Within three short months, though, the salutation had reverted to [Insult].

Do police officers sometimes misuse their power and authority in the pursuit of doing good? Of course. Does the community sometimes expect them to do exactly that? Absolutely. Where, then, are the boundaries, and what can be done to smooth the rough edges of conflict between citizens and law enforcement? Later in this book you will see that many police agencies have taken seriously their responsibility to nurture the good officer and help her succeed in a positive police environment. And this is a critical undertaking because the cumulative negative effect of just one bad police-citizen interaction can be devastating. As Mark Moore noted at the end of his interview with a brutal and corrupt New York City police officer in 1997:

> I had the sense that this one cop could single-handedly wipe out the day-to-day diligent efforts of hundreds of

officers trying to establish better working relationships in communities. My heart sank as I realized how vulnerable the overall legitimacy of the system was to the destructive influence of a relatively small number of bad encounters between officers and citizens.

DISCUSSION QUESTIONS

1. For police officers, what is the meaning of Nietzsche's caution that "Those who fight the monster need to take care that it does not turn them into monsters"?
2. In the aftermath of the terrorist attacks of September 11, 2001, what limits should be placed on police authority to stop, detain, or interrogate citizens?
3. In the aftermath of the terrorist attacks of September 11, 2001, are there circumstances under which the police should be given broad authority to use race or ethnicity in developing probable cause to stop, detain, or interrogate people? What are those circumstances?
4. In an effort to keep cities safe, some police departments have established task forces or teams dedicated to "high-intensity" enforcement of certain laws or quality-of-life violations. What characteristics distinguish a highly motivated and productive police unit from a group of vigilantes functioning outside the constraints of law?

chapter **6**

THE FAILURE OF LAW ENFORCEMENT MANAGEMENT

To the Citizen: As you read this chapter, consider the notion of customer service as it relates to the police in your community. If you have a complaint about a product or service from a company you do business with, a manager will often take steps to correct the problem. Would you expect the same from police leaders? When police corruption scandals occur, news videos usually show frontline officers being arrested and taken to court. Should other members of the department be held responsible as well? Who are they? Why should they be held responsible if they were not directly involved?

To the Police Officer: As you read this chapter, consider several of the high-profile scandals that have erupted in policing over the past few years. What has caused them? When a department comes under scrutiny, at what level is the blame usually placed? In your experience, do police leaders do an effective job of accepting responsibility for the actions of their people? What about accepting responsibility for their own actions? Do you think police officers (and police leaders) should speak out publicly when other members of the profession engage in misbehavior?

THE ROLE OF THE ORGANIZATION

When someone decides to report a problem with the police, they will likely describe some form of dissatisfaction with a uniformed member of the agency. This is to be expected, since the police department employees most directly in contact with citizens are the frontline folks holding ranks such as patrol officer, deputy, and trooper. Variously described as "grunts," "mud marines," or simply the "cop on the street," they are the people a law enforcement agency tasks with delivering police services to the community.

Most police organizations have some formal investigative process they follow once a personnel complaint is received. First, a statement will likely be taken from the citizen. Then independent witnesses will be sought. At some point the officer may be asked to account for his or her actions, and the subsequent investigation will examine all available evidence. All of these steps and others will be employed in an effort to prove or disprove the citizen's allegation, but they overlook a very important element: the role the organization itself may have played in causing or allowing the behavior that is the focus of the complaint.

Nonetheless, officers cannot be absolved of responsibility for their actions. Absolutely not. However, as law enforcement leaders take the easy route of investigating, disciplining, and sometimes firing uniformed cops for violating department rules or engaging in inappropriate behavior, they would be wise to cast an eye at the organization itself. Without question, if an officer is found to have engaged in misconduct, he or she should be held responsible for it. But what did the department do about the last seven similar complaints against this officer? What kind of training or counseling did the officer receive? And, most important, how much did managers in the agency know about what was really going on out on the street? In short, where were the bosses?

In 1996 the U.S. Department of Justice convened the National Symposium on Police Integrity in Washington, D.C. A number of practitioners, educators, politicians, and community leaders, including Chief Ross Swope of the United States Supreme Court, were in attendance. Commenting with simple eloquence on what he saw as the most pressing contemporary challenge to American law enforcement, Chief Swope said, "The major cause of the lack of integrity in American police officers is mediocrity." Interestingly enough, he was not describing law enforcement personnel as mediocre. Instead, he defined mediocrity as the failure of organizations and leaders to hold officers responsible and accountable.

In his view, mediocrity is a function of lazy and excessively tolerant supervisors.

Look at it this way. If you happen to work for IBM or some other private-sector organization, you will likely be asked to meet with your manager periodically to set some work-related goals. Most reputable companies routinely use this approach because it gives both the worker and the supervisor an agreed-upon projection of what they can expect in terms of productivity over, say, the next six to twelve months. Such planning sessions have many potential benefits, including the opportunity for a manager to recognize good work and then deliver praise and other rewards to deserving subordinates.

But let's suppose that at the end of the six- to twelve-month period, you have fallen short of your stated goals. What happens then? First, people in the organization will likely want to talk with you to determine why you didn't perform up to expectations. But the inquiry will not stop there because IBM, like any other reputable private-sector organization, will want information from at least one other person directly connected to you and your shortfall: your supervisor.

In this discussion with your supervisor, the powers that be at IBM will ask whether she knew, over the past six to twelve months, that you were failing. They will also question her about what she did during that period to help you succeed. Did she provide the feedback you needed? The logistical support? The training? The guidance? IBM's position, in other words, will be very simple: You or anyone else who falls short of agreed-upon goals is not working in a vacuum, and your supervisor should have known about—and done something to resolve—the problem before it was too late. As far as IBM is concerned, supervisors are responsible for helping other people do their jobs. When the subordinate fails, the supervisor has failed as well.

Police organizations don't look at things in quite the same way. Historically, law enforcement leaders have not hesitated to criticize the problem behavior of officers on the street, but most often, the "blame game" stops at that level. When a scandal breaks, people at the top of the organization immediately target folks on the front line as the "root of all evil" but rarely look higher in the organization or take managers to task for the failings of their subordinates. Most often, in other words, police leaders, unlike their counterparts in the private sector, flatly reject the notion that supervisors have a responsibility for the actions of their people. This chore is often left to others outside the police department.

THE ROLE OF SUPERVISION

In the early 1990s a corruption scandal erupted in the New York Police Department (NYPD). This is not an uncommon event, unfortunately, but this case was made especially shocking by the brazenness of the criminal behavior of some outlaw police officers. According to investigative reports and court testimony, by the time these rogue officers were taken into custody, their crimes (individually or as a group) included robbery, assault, larceny, burglary, and narcotics trafficking. And although a relatively small number of cops were ultimately found to have been involved, their actions painted a sordid picture of the entire organization.

In response, in 1992 the Commission to Investigate Allegations of Police Corruption and the Anti-Corruption Procedures of the Police Department was formed. Chaired by Judge Milton Mollen, this investigative body (popularly known as the Mollen Commission) was charged with examining and reporting on the scandal. Their work culminated in a scathing report published in 1995 that highlighted a range of problem areas that contributed to the then-current state of affairs, but this time management ranks were not spared. For example, in describing the actions of supervisors in the units and precincts where the officers at the heart of the scandal were assigned, the Mollen Commission used the phrase "willful blindness." In other words, the commission noted, these managers had to have been willfully blind to have overlooked what was taking place virtually in their presence. In their view, there was simply no other reasonable explanation. It is important to keep in mind that the misbehaviors of the problem officers involved in this scandal did not consist of subtle violations of obscure regulations in the NYPD rule book. Much to the contrary. These officers were ultimately convicted of criminal acts committed in such blatant fashion that any reasonable, rational person would have reason to ask "Where were the bosses?"

The myopia of some police supervisors in the scandal was never more evident than in the case of Michael Dowd, a former officer widely recognized as the ringleader of the band of out-of-control cops. Beginning in 1985 and spanning a period of some six years, the NYPD had received sporadic information suggesting that Dowd was a "dirty" cop. But despite opening no fewer than twenty cases directly or tangentially involving him, they were unable to make a case against him. Dowd was ultimately arrested in 1992 by the Suffolk County, New York, Police Department on drug-related charges, and when he was taken into custody, some interesting things came to light—things that the NYPD had apparently overlooked in its scrutiny of him. For example, at the time of his arrest, Dowd—a New York City police patrolman—was living in a $350,000 house on the north shore of Long Island, New York. In addition, he owned two other houses on Long Island and property in Virginia, and he drove a brand-new cherry red Corvette to work at his precinct every day. Oh, and one more thing . . . he never picked up his paycheck at work.

Where were the supervisors? What about internal affairs? Why didn't somebody ask Dowd how he was managing to live such an opulent lifestyle, especially since he wasn't even picking up his police salary? Even Dowd later expressed open amazement that nobody ever caught on to what he and his cohorts were doing. As someone pointed out, there is a word that accurately describes the manner in which the NYPD handled the many complaints it received about Michael Dowd over the six-year period prior to his arrest by Suffolk County: The word is "duh."

The failure of management to take responsibility for the behavior of subordinates is not confined to New York City. In the early 1990s in Louisiana, for example, federal law enforcement officials estimated that 10 to 15 percent of New Orleans police officers were actively engaged in criminal behavior. During this same period, though, not a single New Orleans cop received an unsatisfactory performance evaluation. But in this case, like many others, it is impossible to focus all the blame on line officers for an out-of-control police department. One deputy chief who left the agency around that time had never earned more than $50,000 in any single year over the course of his career yet was able to retire as a multimillionaire. The bulk of his fortune was gained from personal contracts with a gaming business in Las Vegas, which paid him to place gambling devices in a variety of establishments in New Orleans. He then paid police officers a small sum for each such device they could get installed in bars on their posts.

As the horrific Rampart scandal continues to unfold in the Los Angeles Police Department (LAPD), it is becoming apparent that in this disgraceful case, too, supervisors and managers failed to do their jobs as they should have. In its interim report, the LAPD Board of Inquiry into the Rampart Area Corruption Incident expressed its views this way:

> Essentially, many of the problems found by this BOI (Board of Inquiry) boil down to people failing to do their jobs with a high level of consistency and integrity. Unfortunately, we found this to be true at all levels of the organization, including top managers, first line supervisors and line personnel. (Board of Inquiry, Los Angeles Police Department, Executive Summary, Rampart Area Corruption Incident, March 1, 2000, p. 13)

The board identified the failure of employees to follow established LAPD procedures as a particularly discouraging problem, adding that the situation was made even worse by supervisors and managers who did not oversee the work of their subordinates. One reason for this failure, the board noted, was a personnel evaluation system seen as having little or no credibility at any level of the organization.

In making a comparison to corruption scandals in other cities, the BOI report was very specific in attributing the problems in the Rampart Division to a breakdown in frontline management. To help remedy the situation, the board called for improvement in the selection criteria, expertise, and deployment of field supervisors. One specific recommendation would require that sergeant candidates have five years of experience, with at least three of those years in a uniform assignment.

The BOI also noted a widespread perception within the Los Angeles Police Department that there are dual disciplinary standards, one for captains and above and the other for lieutenants and below. It is thus noteworthy that when LAPD Chief Bernard Parks released the interim report in March 2000, he did not propose taking any action against high-ranking officials identified as having failed in their management responsibilities. He also rejected suggestions that he resign to take responsibility for the department-wide lapses.

This refusal to fix responsibility at upper levels of management did not come as a surprise to Gary Fullerton, a former

LAPD detective and a lawyer. In an interview in the *New York Times* (Cannon, October 1, 2000), he noted:

> [F]or a long time, there's been a wink and a nod. That's why we have a war on crime. The people want the criminals caught. The chief wants them caught. The supervisors of the officers want them caught. The politicians want them caught. It's the system. But when something happens, it's the officer. The system goes all out to get him. (p. 62)

After the long nightmare of the Michael Dowd scandal in the early 1990s, the New York City Police Department issued a report identifying a range of similar supervisory failures in its own ranks ("Rooting Out Corruption; Building Organizational Integrity in the New York City Police Department," 1995). This report details a series of focus groups conducted with precinct commanders in 1994, including one in which they were asked to identify the most prominent management weaknesses troubling them. They identified familiarity between sergeants and the police officers they were supposed to supervise as a major problem and attributed the problem to four factors:

1. The closeness in age of most new sergeants to the officers they are required to supervise
2. A lack of seasoning and street experience among many new sergeants
3. The chronic practice, caused by periodic shortages of other patrols, to use sergeants as just another radio unit to respond to 911 calls
4. The inadequate training

The views of the precinct commanders did not come as a surprise to patrol officers and supervisors on the street. In a survey conducted in 1994, the overwhelming majority of uniformed NYPD members at the rank of lieutenant and below took the position that today's frontline supervisors are not strong enough. Of those who responded to the survey, 66.6 percent agreed with the following statement: "Sergeants do not have enough confidence to take charge of many situations on the street."

When police administrators discipline an officer for violating a rule or engaging in misconduct but don't take into account the behavior of the larger organization and its managers, they have failed that officer, the department, and the community. Individuals who provide guidance and direction from the top of the organization have a powerful impact on the manner in which the agency will perform, because they are the ones who form and articulate the overall vision for the department. Employees at every rank and position look to them for guidance, so when they equivocate or, worse yet, remain silent on issues buffeting law enforcement, this behavior amounts to a virtual abdication of leadership responsibility. Those at the top of the pyramid have a bully pulpit, and it is imperative that it be used to let others—both inside and outside the department—know where the organization and its administrators stand on key issues facing both the police and the community.

SILENCE ACROSS THE RANKS

When police officers are asked why there is so much reluctance to speak out about other cops who have engaged in unprofessional conduct, there is often a lengthy pause, followed by the observation that "Policing is no different from most other professions. Have you ever tried to get a doctor to testify against an inept doctor?" Good point. But in law enforcement, a profession deeply imbued with the public trust, it seems illogical that many leaders appear incapable of breaking free from the shackles of the code of silence that is so damaging to organizations and individuals alike. As evidence, simply ask a police chief to comment publicly about misbehavior— even videotaped misbehavior—by an officer from another jurisdiction. He will not do it. The reasons a police chief will cite for remaining mute on such matters might include the following:

1. I don't really know the whole story (what might have caused it).
2. It's really none of my business (it didn't happen in my agency).
3. I have to work with this guy (the other chief) in the future.
4. I have my own problems, and I don't want to turn the spotlight on them.
5. The media are unfair and biased and are out to harm law enforcement.

What is particularly interesting about the alibis police chiefs use to avoid commenting on misbehavior in the ranks of law enforcement is their stark similarity to the alibis police officers use when they refuse to speak out against another officer who may, for example, have used excessive force in making an arrest:

1. I don't really know the whole story (what the citizen might have done to deserve the treatment he or she is receiving).
2. It's really none of my business (I'm not involved, and I'd like to keep it that way).
3. I have to work with this guy (the other police officer) in the future. (In fact, I might even have to rely on him for physical backup when I'm in a jam.)
4. I have my own problems, and I don't want to turn the spotlight on them. (I've made some mistakes in my career, and I don't need the sergeant or internal affairs snooping around my backyard.)
5. The media are unfair and biased and are out to harm law enforcement.

When corruption issues arise in the ranks of a police department, the leaders of that agency have an absolute expectation that officers will speak out about it. In fact, police chiefs will say, when officers remain silent in the face of unprofessional conduct, that silence amounts to nothing less than tacit approval of the misbehavior. They have a point, but law enforcement leaders cannot reasonably expect others to speak out unless they themselves are willing to do so first. Line officers put themselves at considerable risk when they expose misconduct. It only stands to reason that chiefs and sheriffs should be willing to endure those same risks.

In terms of frustration, difficulty, and complexity, though, few jobs compare to that of a police department midrank supervisor. They are the people who are responsible for taking in the words and policies of top management, interpreting them, and making them come to life for their subordinates. Few assignments, frankly, are more daunting and thankless than those of the patrol sergeant or shift lieutenant because they are "slugging it out" every day in the bowels of the organization. They are the bosses who best understand that the formal rules developed and handed down from the top of the organization are often very different from the informal rules followed and endorsed by officers on the street. In fact, they know that where those informal rules of the street conflict with the formal rules of the agency, the informal rules will often prove to be the more powerful and persuasive.

There is one other important way in which police departments fail their officers, and it often links directly to dissatisfaction in the community and consequent citizen complaints. Police actions on the street derive from the policies made at the top of the organization, so when leaders tell their officers to practice "zero tolerance," the message is interpreted as "We want you to make these problems go away." From that message, cops assume that bosses have given them the authority to make mass arrests and use extreme force under certain circumstances, and, unless department leaders have established boundaries for them, officers will take increasingly greater liberties. According to Jerry Sanders, retired chief of police in San Diego, California (*New York Times*, April 16, 1999), before long they can become virtually indiscriminate in their use of the summons or an arrest.

In an interview with Peterson, (*New York Times*, April 21, 1999), New Jersey Governor Christine Todd Whitman spoke directly to this issue in her comments on the reasons behind racial profiling in the patrol ranks of the New Jersey State Police. She put it this way:

> While no official policy permitting such racial profiling existed, *management styles, coaching of state troopers by superiors and a system that rewarded both aggressive ticket-writing and drug seizures* had combined to create an atmosphere that went beyond simple racism to a problem that is more complex than we first realized. (p. 1)

In the New Jersey State Police, in other words, there was a tacit understanding that to be seen as a successful trooper and to advance in the organization, it was important to produce drug arrests and write large numbers of traffic tickets. And, as outlined in Chapter 5, this philosophy was emphasized clearly, repeatedly, and in a number of different ways in the organization. In such a culture, in which high numbers of arrests and drug seizures lead to outstanding performance evaluations, even citizen complaints are, perversely, looked on as an indicator of success. As one high-ranking member of a different state police agency once said to a room full of in-service troopers, "If you don't have a few citizen complaints in your file, people at the top of the organization don't think you are doing your job."

In Manatee County, Florida, an investigation of the special Delta drug enforcement unit of the sheriff's office has led to revelations that members of this group routinely lied on police reports, handed out cocaine to helpful informants, and planted drugs on victims and in victims' homes in order to use seizure laws to confiscate their cars and other property. So far, the corruption in the unit has led to one hundred charges being dropped against sixty-seven defendants. Pointing to wholesale failure of management, an editorial in the *St. Petersburg Times* ("Tarnished Police Trust," June 23, 2000) made the following observations:

> How do police organizations get out of control? It has to do with leadership and supervision. When emphasis is put on bottom-line measures such as a high volume of arrests, respecting constitutional limits can go out the window. In Manatee County, one agent claimed that Delta members didn't have to abide by the regular rules. That attitude develops when a command is less concerned about innocent people being harassed and arrested than about falling crime rates. (p. 2)

DISCUSSION QUESTIONS

1. If a police agency experiences a scandal involving both high-ranking and lower-level officers, who should be punished more severely? Why?
2. Even though a police leader may not have been personally involved in the misconduct of officers under her command, under what circumstances should she be held responsible?
3. What factors may combine to make it difficult for police leaders to speak out openly about corruption or misconduct in the law enforcement profession?
4. Under what circumstances can organizational commendations and rewards for highly productive police officers be a problem?

chapter **7**

WHO WILL POLICE THE POLICE?

To the Citizen: If you have ever made a complaint against a police officer, how do you feel about the way you were received and treated? And if you have never made a complaint, how do you perceive police openness and willingness to receive feedback or criticism from citizens? As you read this chapter, consider whether you think a law enforcement agency is ever capable of investigating itself. Should citizens be given formal authority to oversee the police in their communities?

To the Police Officer: As you read this chapter, consider the role of internal affairs in any police agency. Should it be reactive or proactive in nature? Why? Do you have faith in the way a law enforcement agency investigates wrongdoing by its employees? Do you think citizens trust this process? When a police department fails to adequately police itself, what other options are available to root out and correct misbehavior? What is your view on such things as civilian-police review boards?

Do you have a complaint about your accommodations in a hotel? Assuming your stay was in a reputable facility, simply contact the manager. Almost immediately, people will fall all over themselves to resolve the problem and make sure you return to patronize their facility again. Chances are someone at the corporate level will follow up to make sure you have been satisfied, and occasionally you won't be charged for your stay. A similar approach is used in almost all service industries because the survival of the service companies depends on the goodwill and patronage of . . . well . . . you, their customers.

In fact, most competent organizations regularly survey clients to see if there is a way to do things better. Chief executives in the private sector understand the value of such information because it tends to provide an important snapshot of "how we're doing" from the point of view of the customer. Some retail companies even go so far as to hire mystery shoppers to go into their stores or hotels to act like customers and then provide an objective evaluation of the experience.

Do you have a complaint about a police officer? Don't expect the same type of response. In many cases, when a citizen expresses an interest in filing a complaint against a police officer, the citizen is made to feel like he or she has done something wrong. In some departments, a request for information about filing a complaint is immediately met with a stern warning emphasizing the prospect of being sued or criminally charged for lying, followed by the presentation of a formal complaint document detailing the penalties for making a false statement.

Yes, it is important that citizens understand the gravity of making a false accusation against a police officer. But does it have to be the first thing a citizen is confronted with? In the face of such a rigid, unwelcoming approach, many people will simply walk away. And that is a tremendous loss to the multitude of thoughtful police leaders who are trying to bring about positive change in law enforcement. First of all, it is an example of shoddy customer service. But, more important, it is a missed opportunity to learn about potential problems. Why do police departments make it so difficult for a citizen to be heard? And why don't they aggressively seek out information about officers who misbehave?

TESTING THE POLICE

Remember the old saying "Where there's smoke, there's fire"? Well, for most police agencies, this motto is an accurate characterization of the way internal affairs personnel see their role. In other words, if a problem surfaces ("If we see smoke"), we will investigate ("We will look for the fire"). But some would argue that when a police department waits until there is smoke before it starts looking for problems, it has waited far too long. To stretch the fire department metaphor just a bit further, if internal affairs investigators, like firefighters, wait for an alarm to sound before responding and dealing with a problem, the situation may already be out of control before it is even detected.

In contrast, some large city police departments (Baltimore, Los Angeles, New Orleans, and New York, for example) have opted for an aggressive, proactive approach to internal investigations. These agencies, using different forms of compliance testing, find it beneficial to periodically evaluate the behavior of all departmental employees. In some cases a targeted test, in response to a pattern of allegations or instances of misconduct, would be aimed at a specific officer or group of officers identified as involved in wrongdoing. Random testing, on the other hand, is intended to check on the behavior of an officer who may have been chosen simply because his badge or payroll number happened to be randomly selected on a particular day.

Proponents of proactive internal affairs investigations say the process is highly effective, and, in fact, very few officers fail random integrity tests. One of the greatest benefits of an aggressive approach to this issue, supporters say, is that it tends to keep everyone's behavior in line—even those who are not tested— because all officers know they could be subjected to a test at any time in the course of their duties. And besides, they add, if officers are doing their jobs the way they are supposed to, they have nothing to fear from a proactive integrity test.

Very few law enforcement professionals are troubled by the use of tests when there are indications that a targeted officer may be involved in misbehavior. But when it comes to aggressive internal affairs policies that would include the use of random or periodic tests for all personnel, the lines are clearly drawn. Many see such testing as a violation of rights and decry the diminished trust that is certain to follow. (Never mind that many agencies already require random drug screening, a form of random integrity testing.) Generally speaking, police officers tend to oppose surreptitious examination of their actions, in any form, regardless of who may be doing it.

In late 1999 a television station in Dallas, Texas, decided to test the willingness of agencies to provide information about the procedure for a citizen to make a complaint about police officers. In doing so, it partnered with the Police Complaint Center at Florida State University, a group with substantial experience in conducting the types of tests the TV station was undertaking. The exercise, which was simple and straightforward, involved a young man (wired with a camera and microphone) walking into a number of police stations in the Dallas–Fort Worth area and asking, "How can I make a complaint against a police officer?" Pretty simple. Right?

The young man conducting the test visited approximately forty police agencies as part of the survey, and, for the most part, he was treated professionally. When he asked for information about making a complaint, he was most often given the forms he needed, provided information on the steps he needed to follow, or invited to meet with a supervisor to discuss the matter. But a positive response was not universal. In several cases (captured on video), he was threatened with arrest, told he would get a better response if he "came in bloodied up," or otherwise denied access to the information he was seeking. Remember, this is a citizen seeking readily available information from a public servant.

News about this investigative report leaked out before it was televised, prompting several Dallas–Fort Worth area police leaders to express outrage at this sting operation, crying foul at the techniques being used. (As an aside, it was difficult to ignore the irony of hearing professionals who use stings to capture citizens all the time complain about being the targets of a sting.) And, of course, the stories began to circulate. First, word went around that the people conducting the test were committing traffic violations so they would be pulled over to "set up" the police officer. This was untrue. Next was the rumor that the investigative team members were listening to police radio frequencies so they could track officers. Also untrue.

When the report aired, most thoughtful police officers tended to agree that the examples of unprofessional conduct they saw televised were an embarrassment to the profession. But some would not be swayed; they held that the program did not show the outtakes (the segments of video that were edited out), implying that there must be some film footage lying on the studio floor that would hold the key to the inappropriate conduct shown on TV. This, of course, ignores the simple fact that every officer shown behaving unprofessionally could have avoided embarrassment by simply following department policy and giving the young man the information he was seeking.

Nevertheless, a few unhappy police chiefs continued to complain that, like all media events, this one was biased. What many of them did not know, though, was that twice before a very similar exercise had been undertaken in the Dallas–Fort Worth area, but with one major difference: The earlier tests had been conducted by police commanders themselves. The Institute for Law Enforcement Administration (ILEA) (formerly the Southwestern Law Enforcement Institute), located in Plano, Texas, conducts an annual eight-week management college for police leaders from around the United States. In 1994, and again in 1996, students in this program were given the opportunity to measure customer service in law enforcement by going out to area police agencies and asking—get this now—how they could make a complaint against a police officer. Does this question sound familiar?

When the participants in the Institute for Law Enforcement Administration exercise began their survey, the rules were simple: They had to wear civilian clothes, they could not identify themselves as police officers, and they could visit any police or sheriff's department they chose. After asking how to make a complaint, they were to complete a form evaluating the experience from a customer service point of view and then orally report their experience to their peers in the management college class. Like the investigative TV report in late 1999, the results of the ILEA surveys showed that the majority of contacts were handled in a satisfactory manner, with some labeled as very professional. One student described his experience in this way: "I was treated like someone very important. I have never been treated better. The welcome and treatment were better than when I've visited departments that knew I was an officer. I was impressed."

On the other end of the spectrum were agencies that did not fare so well. In a few cases ILEA students were met with outright rudeness, insensitivity, and suspicion, but none were treated as poorly as one participant, who reported his experience in this way: "Very unfriendly. The officer stated that in order to file a complaint I would have to talk to the mayor. However, the process was that if a citizen complained to an officer, they just beat the hell out of them to ensure there are no more complaints. Upon answering the locked door, the officer stood in the doorway and refused to let me enter." It is probably safe to assume that citizens do not complain about the police very much in that community. At least not more than once.

If you listen closely, you will discover a common theme when law enforcement officers complain about the "biased" nature of investigative journalism. It goes this way: "Those" people don't have any police experience, so they don't know what it is really like out there. This argument, of course, fails when police professionals (as in the ILEA experience) are the ones reporting rude and unprofessional treatment. It is noteworthy that, at the beginning of the study, some ILEA participants expressed concerns about entrapping an officer with a provocative question. In the end, though, most agreed there was genuine value in learning that, sometimes, citizens may be telling the truth when they say they have been poorly treated or when they have been made to feel like intruders for simply seeking information or guidance from a law enforcement agency.

In the movie *The Doctor*, the lead character (played by William Hurt) was a high-powered heart surgeon with very little regard for patients and hospital staff, whom he treated as merely incidental to his successful practice and career. With the discovery of a cancerous tumor in his throat, though, the formerly powerful and self-assured physician found himself on the outside looking in, a patient in a system that he quickly found to be unfeeling, cold, and virtually impenetrable. In this new experience, credentials and professional status meant nothing, and the doctor learned how it felt to be in the position of any other frightened human being facing surgery while being confronted by a system that treated him as though he were transparent.

To his credit, the doctor used his experience as an outsider to change the way he interacted with patients and staff and to help new interns look at the field of medicine from the viewpoint of the patient. In the ILEA customer service surveys, police leaders had an opportunity to see how it really feels to come up against the monolith of policing from the perspective of the average citizen. The results reveal that there may be merit in forcing police officers occasionally to walk in the shoes of the frustrated citizen trying to generate a caring response from a sometimes cold, faceless bureaucracy.

Like the experience of William Hurt in *The Doctor*, the "How do I make a complaint?" exercise undertaken by management classes at the Institute for Law Enforcement Administration has always been far less about testing the complaint-acceptance procedures of the agencies visited and far more about giving police practitioners the opportunity to experience how it feels to ask for provocative yet public information when nobody knows you are a cop. By and large, participants in this exercise over the years have agreed that it is an uncomfortable feeling. When that same exercise was conducted in early 2002, by the way, most agencies—as usual—handled the request for information very professionally. In a few cases, though, ILEA course participants were dismayed at the treatment they received; in one instance, a student was told that in order to receive information on how to make a complaint, he would have to provide his "full name, date of birth, Social Security number, home address, and home phone number." According to the police agency representative, that information would be "entered into a database."

One interesting aspect of the "we-they" state of mind affecting relationships between police officers and citizens is that it is so obvious to those on the outside looking in and so invisible to those on the inside looking out. Citizens sometimes experience and complain about police behavior they describe as rude, arrogant, or unprofessional, only to hear police leaders characterize these same actions as businesslike and professional. As a result, many frustrated citizens simply give up on complaining. But for one group of people—retired and former police officers—it is an earth-shaking experience to come up against an impenetrable law enforcement bureaucracy for the first time as an outsider. Up to that point, many of them—bless their hearts—still had innocent faith in the system, and it was only when they found themselves treated like regular people that the light finally came on. As one retired officer with a minor complaint about police behavior said recently, "I can't believe they treated me that way." Indeed. Welcome to the club.

THE MOVE TOWARD "CUSTOMER SERVICE"

Let's face it: Police agencies have a lot of work to do to make themselves customer-friendly when it comes to accepting feedback about their officers' behavior. In early 2000, in Kansas City, Missouri, the city auditor cited a number of restrictions that unduly limited who can file complaints as well as when and where they can be filed. Pointing out that "Filing a citizen complaint alleging police misconduct should be easier," he suggested eight strategies for improving the process, including recommendations that the number of complaint intake locations be increased and that complaint materials be made more readily available. He also suggested that intake personnel forward *all* complaints to the Office of Civilian Complaints. Previously, complaint forms were available at only eight locations in Kansas City, and anonymous complaints, those filed by someone under age eighteen without an adult's signature or those filed more than sixty days after the alleged incident could be rejected.

In New Orleans, Louisiana, when Richard Pennington became police superintendent in 1994, one of his first official acts was to completely disband the internal affairs unit. In its place, he established a public integrity division and—here's the key—moved it out into the community. Prior to that change, any citizen wanting to complain about a New Orleans police officer had to physically appear at police headquarters, ask directions to internal affairs, and take an elevator to an upper floor—a process that tended to dissuade many from stepping forward to make a complaint. By making the process easier for citizens and, at least figuratively, opening the doors and windows of the department, Pennington was able to let people know that he was actively seeking feedback on how his agency was doing.

When Charles Moose was appointed police chief in Montgomery County, Maryland, in 1999, he instituted several changes in the way his agency would accept complaints from citizens. For example, complaint forms can now be picked up and submitted at community centers, whereas in the past they were available only at the five district stations. As a result of the new initiative, complaints in the first three months of 2000 more than doubled compared to the same period in 1999 (from 80 to 176). Overall, complaints rose from 396 in 1998 to 452 in 1999. In an interview with the *Washington Post*, Moose attributed the increase to his agency's encouraging people to report problems and noted, "It just means we are doing more."

But many citizens remain unconvinced that police departments are capable of adequately investigating themselves. In Montgomery County, for example, of the 24 percent of complaints deemed worthy of investigation by internal affairs, the largest share were the forty-three that alleged excessive or inappropriate use of force. Only one of these complaints was ultimately sustained. Of the remainder, investigators determined thirteen to be unfounded, exonerated the officers in twelve others, ruled against sustaining five complaints, and closed seven cases administratively. Five cases were still pending as of June 2000.

In early 2000 the Albany, New York, Police Department released statistics showing a decline in citizen complaints over the past several years and pointed to improved professionalism as the reason for the drop. But others in the community did not agree; they cited a widespread belief that there is little point in making a report, since misconduct complaints are not thoroughly investigated anyway. As evidence, they point to the department's own records, which show that in 1998 only seven of eighty formal complaints were sustained. A department spokesperson did little to clarify the situation when she explained, "Just because things are not sustained doesn't mean they necessarily didn't happen. But if they are sustained, it generally means the complaint occurred as the complainant described." Huh?

CIVILIAN-POLICE REVIEW

Maybe it is time for private citizens to seek and be given a more active role in overseeing their police departments. Unfortunately, anyone with a mind toward proposing this solution in his or her community had better be prepared for a fight. Citizen oversight groups (or civilian-police review boards) are anathema to most police leaders; the most commonly cited objection is that citizens do not understand what police work entails and are therefore unsuited to judge the actions of an officer. And therein lies the rub. If, on the one hand, citizens lack the insight necessary to judge the police, and, on the other hand, police show little enthusiasm for investigating themselves, who will police the police? Where can an aggrieved citizen turn for satisfaction?

The answer may lie in some form of civilian complaint review, but, historically, according to Dr. Samuel Walker of the University of Nebraska at Omaha, there has never been an effective system for oversight or review of police actions. In a speech at the Southwestern Law Enforcement Institute shortly after the Rodney King event, Walker pointed to a small percentage of police officers nationwide who seem to attract the majority of complaints in the communities where they work but who also seem to operate with impunity. Citing statistics current at the time, Walker noted that in the Los Angeles Police Department, 2 percent of the sworn officers accounted for 28 percent of complaints against the agency. Similar conditions existed elsewhere, with 10 percent of Boston officers receiving 45 percent of the complaints and 2 percent of sworn police officers generating 50 percent of the citizen complaints in Kansas City, Missouri.

Clearly, administrators and internal affairs personnel need to refocus their efforts to effectively deal with officers repeatedly mentioned in citizen complaints. Failure to adequately oversee and correct problem behavior is a major management shortcoming, but one that continues to haunt law enforcement today. In the ever-widening scandal in the Rampart Division of the Los Angeles Police Department, it was recently pointed out that of the officers named in a variety of offenses, including perjury, assault, and tampering with evidence, twenty of them have been the subject of more than one hundred lawsuits in the past. Several have been sued more than ten times each. In light of this information, a right-thinking, rational person would want to know why these officers were still permitted to work in high-risk, special assignments. In short, where were the bosses?

One police leader who has broken new ground in the management of civilian complaints in his agency is Sheriff Leroy D. Baca in Los Angeles County, California. In April 2000 he submitted a proposal to the Los Angeles County Board of Governors recommending dramatically enhanced civilian oversight of his department. The proposal, which was approved in July 2000 and began work in October 2001, created the Office of Independent Review (OIR) with a staff of six attorneys with criminal law and civil rights backgrounds. Empowered to review all internal investigations in the Los Angeles County Sheriff's Department, OIR works closely with the Office of Internal Affairs and the Office of Internal Criminal Investigation. To many, it is a historic and precedent-setting move and a significant break from most major police organizations. Several other cities, including San Francisco and Chicago, have some form of civilian oversight of police, but none is as far-reaching as Baca's proposal.

Some groups traditionally seen as adversaries of the police have spoken in support of the proposal, saying it will add credibility and independence to the oversight process. Sheriff Baca agrees but says the proposal is nothing more than a way of advancing his view of reform while deflecting critics who have long argued that the police cannot police themselves. Once the system is in place, the Office of Independent Review will make recommendations concerning which deputies should be disciplined or prosecuted, although the sheriff will retain the authority to make the final decision on each case.

Recently in Louisville, Kentucky, members of the police department, outraged that the chief of police had been dismissed by the city manager, began a series of protests across the community. As with many movements, there was the obligatory rally at city hall, but the police protest in Louisville apparently made itself felt in another distinctive way: The police stopped writing tickets and enforcing certain laws. Much to their dismay, the slowdown may have backfired on them because community leaders and citizens began wondering aloud about the actions of their police. "When the president decides to replace the head of the Joint Chiefs of Staff, the army doesn't march on Washington," noted one resident. "What makes the police think they are any different?" And as one educator at the University of Louisville observed, "The police have forgotten who works for whom."

This is a central issue in the discussion of how police departments handle citizen complaints. Ultimately, police officers are public servants. In a democracy, the police are supposed to be in place and responsive to the citizens who employ them, and citizens have an absolute right to be heard and tended to when there are questions about the behavior—or misbehavior—of the police.

Despite the forward-looking approach of Sheriff Leroy Baca and a few others, many law enforcement personnel long for the "good old days," when people didn't question the police and there was no doubt about who was in charge. Traditionalists would understand and appreciate the crusty old police sergeant working in a rural community who, years ago, knew exactly how to handle people who complained. When one woman kept calling and whining about some problem she was having, the sergeant assigned an officer to go to her house and cut the phone line. The officer did, but the woman apparently figured out how to splice the line together, and her calls began again. Undaunted, the sergeant sent the officer back to the woman's house with new orders: Cut the line again . . . twice. Make the cuts six feet apart, . . . and bring me the six-foot length of phone line.

DISCUSSION QUESTIONS

1. When police agencies decide to test the integrity of their officers, should those tests be proactive or reactive in nature? What is the difference between the two?

2. When a citizen decides to make a complaint about a police officer, what level of customer service should she expect to

receive from the department that employs the officer? Should it be the same as she would receive from, say, a major retail department store?

3. How much authority should be given to civilian-police review boards in the investigation of complaints against the police? Why do some police officers object to civilian oversight of their work?

4. Who will be more likely to generate complaints from citizens, an officer working in a street-enforcement unit in a high-crime neighborhood or a school liaison officer assigned to an upscale suburban area? How should police leaders take into account the differences between the two?

chapter 8

CITIZEN BEHAVIOR SKILLS

To the Citizen: As you read this chapter, consider the last official interaction (if any) you may have had with the police. Were you pleased with the result? Was the outcome affected by any particular behaviors or actions on your part? What were they? Do you disagree with any of the suggestions in this chapter? Which ones? What other citizen behavior skills would you add to this list?

To the Police Officer: Before reading this chapter, bring to mind a positive official interaction you recently had with a citizen and the behaviors that person exhibited. What did the citizen do to help it go well? If an interaction went poorly in the past, what did the citizen do (or not do) to help bring about this outcome? What behavior skills would you recommend to a citizen to increase the likelihood of smooth police-citizen interactions?

For any citizen stopped by a police officer, there is a proven and reliable strategy certain to be of assistance: cooperation. Yes, there are times when it is extremely difficult to keep from telling someone what you *really* think (especially if the other person is wrong), but when it comes to encounters with the police, it is much, much wiser to keep things as cool as possible. If you feel you were stopped or treated inappropriately, you can always complain later, but keeping things as low-key as possible during the actual police-citizen contact should be the goal for every party involved. Knowing that the first few words spoken by either the police or the citizen can have a powerful impact on the interaction that follows, police departments have spent a great deal of time and money training in such things as tactical communication and verbal judo. Citizens, too, must understand that their own actions, words, and attitudes (even tone of voice) can affect the way an encounter eventually plays out.

Police work is dangerous, and officers know that a "routine" encounter can turn very bad, very quickly. As evidence, the U.S. Department of Justice (DOJ) annually compiles and reports data on officers killed in the line of duty. According to the 2001 DOJ report (the most current available), 140 law enforcement officers died as a result of criminal action, including the 71 who perished in the terrorist attacks on September 11, 2001. The other 69 officers died under the following circumstances:

Responses to domestic disturbance calls	10
Traffic pursuits and stops	10
Investigations of drug-related matters	8
Attempts at making other arrests or serving arrest warrants	8
Investigations of suspicious person or circumstances	8
Ambushs (unprovoked attacks)	7
Disturbance calls (bar fights, persons with guns, etc.)	5
Robberies in progress or pursuits of robbery suspects	4
Ambushs (entrapment and premedition)	3
Burglaries in progress or pursuits of burglary suspects	2
Handling, transport, or custody of prisoners	2
Handling mentally deranged persons	2

Further, the DOJ reports that 60 of those officers were killed with firearms, including 45 slain with handguns, 11 with rifles, and 4 with shotguns. The remaining 9 officers were killed with vehicles (7); personal weapons including hands, fists, and feet (1); and a blunt object (1). When they died, 39 officers were wearing body armor, and 16 had attempted to use their weapons but were unable to fire. During the incident causing their deaths, 12 of the slain officers had fired their own weapons, 7 had their weapons stolen from them, and 3 were killed with their own weapons.

Police officers may not be able to cite the exact numbers in the annual law enforcement casualty count, but they remain acutely aware that many of their colleagues are killed or injured in the line of duty each year. As a consequence, well-trained officers can be expected to exhibit strong officer safety skills at all times. There is no question that some of these skills may be perceived as threatening or even questionable from a customer service point of view. But it is important to remember that police officers are always mindful of their safety and the safety of others (both police and citizens) around them.

In Chapter 4, we explored the issue of officer safety, but one last word on the subject is in order. It is important to remember that, intrusive though it may seem, sometimes a police officer has legitimate legal authority to subject you to a pat-down search. Generally, these types of searches are permitted when the officer has reasonable suspicion that you might be carrying a weapon or other contraband, and they are a valid police practice used to help officers ensure their own safety. Do not resist a pat-down search. On the other hand, officers must always be able to explain why they subjected someone to a pat-down. Therefore, if you feel you have been searched without justification, you should later ask to speak with a supervisor for an explanation.

Remember, as well, that a police officer could have any number of legitimate reasons for stopping you. A crime may have been committed nearby, for example, and the perpetrator may still be in the area. Even if you are not a suspect, the police may want to know if you saw or heard anything. In any event, the police officer does not wish to detain you any longer than necessary, so cooperation on your part will always help things to move along quickly.

The best way to avoid an unpleasant encounter with law enforcement is to obey the law and behave appropriately at all times. Toward that end, there are some things you should always keep in mind if you are stopped by the police. These guidelines are described in the following sections.

ALWAYS COOPERATE WITH THE POLICE

Always follow the orders of a police officer. If you feel you were stopped without justification or were treated badly after the stop, you can always complain later. However, citizen noncooperation will always make a bad situation worse. This is excellent advice, by the way, whether you are walking outdoors, driving or riding in a car, or occupying your home.

The issue of cooperation also extends to vehicle searches. This is a highly controversial issue because it involves the fundamental Fourth Amendment right of every citizen to be free from unreasonable searches. But in reality, many motorists have had their vehicles and possessions searched despite refusing permission for the police to do so and, in the process, endured a great deal of humiliation and unnecessary stress. As with all other concerns about police behavior, a formal complaint can be entered after the fact. And in situations involving searches, whether justified or unjustified, officers must always be able to articulate the reasons for their actions.

Under some circumstances a police officer has a legal right to search your vehicle, your person, and even your premises. At other times, though, you must give your consent for a search to take place. On the latter occasions, if you decide to refuse permission, be sure to politely inform the officer.

Never Make Quick or Surreptitious Moves

If you reach for your pocket for identification, an officer (viewing your move from an officer safety point of view) may think you are trying to reach for a weapon. Always keep your hands in sight and open, and reach for your wallet or identification only when directed to do so.

If you are the driver of a motor vehicle, you may be asked to produce a driver's license, auto registration, or insurance card. Before reaching into the glove box, under the seat, or over the visor, always tell the officer where the items are located and that you will be reaching in that direction for them.

Always Provide the Information Requested

To the best of your ability, answer the questions a police officer poses to you. If you doubt whether the questions being asked are legitimate or even legal, you have the option of later on asking to speak with a supervisor for a further explanation or to make a formal complaint. But providing the requested information when asked will help to make the interaction smooth, low-key, and as brief as possible.

Of course, you have no obligation to make admissions or statements that might implicate you. Further, if you happen to be taken into custody, it is always advisable to seek the assistance of an attorney before speaking to the police regarding your case.

Always Remain Respectful

You may feel uncomfortable and even demeaned at times, but remaining polite and respectful through the duration of any encounter is good advice. Police officers are trained to address citizens as "Sir" or "Ma'am." Using these courtesy titles is an excellent suggestion for citizens as well.

Always Keep Your Hands Open and in Plain Sight

When you are talking with a police officer, present yourself in as non-threatening a fashion as possible. One way to do so is to keep your hands out of your pockets and in view throughout the encounter. If you happen to be stopped while driving a car, you should keep your hands on the steering wheel so they are in plain sight.

Avoid "Smart-Aleck," Rude, or Snide Comments

Your blood may be boiling, but using pejorative terms or making comments intended to demean, ridicule, or threaten an officer can work against you in very real ways. For police officers, it is important always to be in full control of police-citizen interactions; officers often view words or actions that might be interpreted as threatening or disrespectful as a challenge to their authority or, even worse, a potential threat to their physical well-being. When that happens, some officers believe it is their immediate responsibility to do whatever it takes to maintain control and to remind the citizen of exactly who is in charge.

Sometimes a citizen can be so disrespectful that an officer may consider him or her to be in violation of the unofficial offenses of "contempt of cop" or "pissing off the police." Definitions of these "crimes" cannot be found in any formal law book, but police officers know they exist, and they have an intuitive sense of what it takes for somebody to qualify. Unfortunately, it may not be possible for a citizen to know he or she is in "contempt of cop" until it is too late, because the exact behaviors that constitute a violation may not be the same for every officer and every situation. After all, some police officers are more patient, tolerant, and experienced than others, and some citizens have better control of their emotions than others.

Sometimes the amount of verbal abuse a police officer is willing to accept may be linked to some other personal characteristics of the citizen. For example, things such as age, race, gender, sexual orientation, attire, and political position may affect how much a cop will put up with. And if the uncooperative person happens to be obviously wealthy or influential, many cops take special pleasure in finding little ways to remind these high-status people of where the power resides in the police-citizen interaction. In other words, a young mom with three kids in the back of a Taurus station wagon who gets stopped for speeding will have her ticket written very quickly so she can be on her way. For the arrogant, young dot.com millionaire in a BMW convertible, though, the same process can take a really, really, *really* long time.

But even in the face of the most severe forms of disrespect, police officers rarely fabricate a criminal charge or violation. Instead, when "contempt of cop" issues come to bear, they usually just result in an officer deciding to make a formal arrest or issue a citation that might have been overlooked if the citizen's attitude had been different. And there is often evidence of this fact in the very words of the arresting officer when he says to a citizen, "Hey, pal, you talked yourself into this."

Finally, some officers view overcoming and punishing disrespect from a citizen as a duty they must perform for the benefit of other officers. In other words, many cops are convinced that if they allow a citizen to get away with being disrespectful, it will make it harder for the next police officer that person comes in contact with. Some have suggested, in fact, that Rodney King's beating was delivered, in part, to send a clear message about how he should behave the next time a police officer tried to stop his vehicle or take him into custody.

WHEN THE POLICE STOP YOUR CAR

If you are driving a car and are pulled over by the police, keep in mind the following:

1. Do not make any quick or furtive movements toward the glove box or under the seats. The officer who pulled you over will be watching you and the interior of your vehicle from the time

he executes the traffic stop. Any rapid or suspicious movement will raise concerns on the officer's part about whether you might be hiding (or reaching for) a weapon or contraband.

2. If you have passengers in your car with you, tell them to stay in the car, remain quiet, and cooperate with the police.

3. Do not get out of your vehicle unless you are ordered to do so. Some officers may perceive your getting out of your car after being stopped as aggressive behavior, and you should avoid doing so. If you are ordered to get out of your car, do so.

4. Always open the driver's side window of your car so you can communicate with the officer. If the traffic stop has taken place at night, turn on the interior light of your vehicle.

5. If the officer asks for anything (license, registration, insurance card) located in the glove box or elsewhere in your car, always tell her where those things are and that you will be reaching into that area for them.

6. If you are issued a traffic summons and asked to sign it, do so. Your signature is merely an acknowledgment that you have received a ticket and not an admission of guilt. If a motorist refuses to sign a ticket, that act alone can result in arrest and additional charges.

Never Resist Arrest

If you are told that you are under arrest, always submit willingly. Psychologically difficult and humiliating though it may be, allow yourself to be handcuffed and remain cooperative. If your arrest is later found to be faulty or otherwise based on insufficient evidence, the charge will be dismissed and you can seek redress through a number of avenues. But an added resisting arrest charge will take precedence over all other matters. Cops do not like to be put in the position of having to overcome physical (or even verbal) resistance, and police department administrators, prosecutors, and judges tend to be very supportive of law enforcement officers in this regard.

Never Interfere in the Arrest of Another Person

Taking someone into custody is a highly risky and potentially explosive situation in which police officers are rightly very conscious of their safety. Consequently, if you do or say anything that may potentially interfere with an officer's ability to safely and quickly arrest someone, you will be viewed as an obstruction and a threat, and you may be arrested yourself. If you are convinced that the other person has been subjected to a wrongful arrest, you may later share your concerns with a police supervisor or even with the court. But you should never get in the way of an arrest out on the street.

WHEN THE POLICE COME TO YOUR HOME

If the police come to your door, the operative word should be, once again, *cooperation*. If the officer is not in uniform and therefore not readily identifiable, be sure to ask for identification in the form of a badge or identification card. Legitimate police officers will never hesitate to provide official credentials to assure you of who they are.

Although there are a few precise conditions under which a police officer may enter your home uninvited ("hot pursuit" and with certain types of warrants, for example), in most cases your residence is absolutely sacrosanct. If the officers at your door do not have a warrant or are not in hot pursuit of someone suspected of committing a crime, you may deny them entry to your home.

SUMMARY

As pointed out earlier, the key to avoiding unhappy interactions with the police is to obey the law at all times. If you are stopped, are interviewed, or otherwise come in official contact with a member of the law enforcement community, though, you should cooperate fully and keep your emotions under control. You should comply with all police officer requests as long as the requests will not place you in danger. If complying with the officer's request may put you at risk in some way, you should ask to speak with a police supervisor immediately.

One of the most valued rights we have as citizens is the freedom to move about at will. Therefore, when we are stopped by a police officer, subjected to a pat-down search, or detained for the purposes of a legitimate interview, this seemingly minor event can be profoundly upsetting. The encounter is less difficult for the police officer, who, after all, may stop or detain numerous people during the course of a single tour of duty. For a citizen who suddenly finds his or her freedom of movement restricted for the first time, though, the process can be stressful, humiliating, and, in some cases, infuriating. Keeping one's composure in such situations can be very difficult; making a concerted effort to do so is absolutely imperative.

A citizen dissatisfied with any form of police service has numerous ways in which to register his or her concerns. Many are outlined and explained in Chapter 9.

DISCUSSION QUESTIONS

1. What is the best way for citizens to avoid any sort of problem interaction with a police officer?

2. Why is it essential for citizens to retain their self-control when interacting with police officers, even in situations where an officer may be wrong?

3. Why do police officers believe it is essential for them to remain in full control of their interactions with citizens? What are some of their concerns?

4. When a citizen is involved in an interaction with a police officer, how can he be sure he doesn't commit the hazy offense of "contempt of cop"?

chapter 9

MAKING A COMPLAINT AGAINST THE POLICE

To the Citizen: As you read this chapter, consider the steps you might follow if you wanted to make a complaint against a police officer. Whom would you speak to? Where would you go for support? If a police department proved unresponsive to you, what other avenues could you follow? If you chose to make a formal complaint against an officer, what information would you need? Where would you obtain it?

To the Police Officer: Before you read this chapter, envision a "problem" police officer with a history of assaultive and corrupt behavior. Should there be a viable system for removing such an employee from a police department? When a citizen makes a complaint about a police officer, is that complaint received in an atmosphere of openness and support? Should it be? If a department fails to adequately discipline employees, should citizens have other avenues to follow in seeking redress? When a citizen makes a complaint, how open and supportive should agencies (and other officers) be?

Despite the historic difficulties involved in carrying forward a complaint about a police officer, citizens have an absolute right—an obligation, really—to do so. And even in the face of the cultural bonds that make policing all that it is (see Chapter 3), most police officers would agree on one irrefutable fact: They do not want problem officers working in the ranks around them. On this point, at least, they are in complete agreement with citizens. Police officers may be reluctant to blow the whistle on one another, but when a bad cop is fired, very little grieving takes place.

Even police union leaders, who have a fiduciary responsibility to stand beside a union member brought up on charges and facing discipline, shed no tears when a problem officer is removed from an agency. In fact, police unions and police administrators are really very close on issues of substance when it comes to running a police department: Both want police officers to be safe, well compensated, and possessed of sufficient job benefits to allow them and their families to live comfortably. In addition, they both want to do whatever they can to improve the lives of the people who live in the communities they serve.

That said, when you begin the process of making a complaint, there are two important rules to keep in mind at all times:

1. Take careful notes as you go through every step of the process. Write down the name, rank, and position of every person you have spoken to; the date and time of each contact; and a synopsis of what each person said. Safeguard the notes, and never turn the originals over to anyone.
2. Remain respectful and polite at all times. You may be angry and justifiably upset, but it is imperative that you keep your emotions under control. Your demeanor will mean a great deal. People are more likely to listen if you state your position in a calm, clear manner.

It is important to remember something else. Police officers, just like private citizens, have certain rights available to them. If you decide to make a complaint, the officer has a right to know the particulars of what you are alleging and to defend herself against them. For this reason, at some point in the process you will likely be asked to put your complaint in writing and to swear to or affirm the truthfulness of what you are saying. And, finally, even if your complaint is found at the end of the investigation to have merit, the officer—just like every other citizen—has the right to appeal.

Keeping in mind, once again, that the best way to avoid any difficulties—and the need for subsequent complaints about the police—is to obey the law and behave appropriately, a citizen can register a complaint in a variety of ways, as described in the following sections.

REGISTER A COMPLAINT WITH THE CHIEF ADMINISTRATOR OF THE ORGANIZATION

You can initiate contact with the chief by telephoning, by sending a letter, or by going into the police department in person. In a major agency, you are unlikely to have an opportunity to meet with the chief directly. But even in small departments, the person at the top may be unwilling to become directly involved for several reasons. First, if the leader is in a politically tenuous situation in the community, he may want to distance himself from any complaints that could further weaken his position. Second, the chief himself may have engaged in the type of behavior you are wanting to complain about or may even be doing so at the present time.

On the other hand, some chiefs—those truly interested in professionalizing the agency—may see your complaint as a potential source of valuable information and will want to take a direct role in seeing it through. Even in these cases, though, the chief may want to distance himself from the actual investigation. Since the person at the top of the organization is often the one who will hand down punishment for a sustained complaint, he may want to stay as objective as possible to avoid any appearance of impropriety, which might jeopardize the eventual outcome. In any case, even if you are able to register your complaint directly with the person at the top, your case will likely be handed off to some other unit or person (internal affairs, for example) for full investigation.

REGISTER A COMPLAINT WITH INTERNAL AFFAIRS

Most police officers view an assignment to internal affairs (IA) with approximately the same degree of enthusiasm as a trip to the dentist's office for a root canal. Whereas many police units— Special Weapons and Tactics (SWAT), canines, bicycle patrol— have more than enough volunteers, IA has usually been the one duty to which a chief has to assign someone. (Some officers would say they have been sentenced to work in IA rather than assigned.) In short, it is usually not a popular detail, and the reason is simple: Officers know they will generally be in IA for only a relatively short period before they are back out on the streets. As a consequence, nobody wants to become known as a cop who enjoys investigating other cops because it won't be long before that "former IA guy" is out there counting on backup and support from the very people he was only recently investigating.

And this perspective is unfortunate because internal affairs units perform an extremely valuable role in a professional law enforcement organization. One of the most important functions is to act as conscience for the agency; like an individual conscience, they remind us that there are boundaries we should not cross and penalties for crossing them. They are also a visible symbol to the community at large that the police are responsive and, in that vein, serve as a conduit for citizen input and concerns.

In large agencies a specific unit may be assigned strictly to IA duties; the Los Angeles, California, Police Department, for example, has approximately three hundred employees assigned to the internal affairs section. In small departments, on the other hand certain supervisors or investigators may take on IA duties as part of their normal activities when a complaint is registered. Either way, a citizen should have some means by which to register a complaint with a unit or person with IA responsibilities. The complaint can usually be made in person, by telephone, or by letter, but, as mentioned earlier, at some point the concerns will likely have to be written down and attested to. Generally, a complaint should be made in writing and sworn to within sixty days after the event occurred; many agencies will accept complaints after that time only for very special reasons.

Incidentally, some police departments (Dallas, Texas, for example) are now using the Internet as another means of receiving both commendations of and complaints about police officers. Citizens can access the agency Web page and contact internal affairs or the public integrity division. To formalize the process, though, the citizen still must both meet with an investigator for a face-to-face interview and sign either the complaint or commendation.

As an aside, the eyes of police officers often light up when they first learn of the possibility of entering commendations or complaints via the Internet. This is one of the reasons for the face-to-face contact with an investigator. Absent the formal meeting, there would be an almost irresistible temptation for a few devious officers to swamp internal affairs with complaints about supervisors they don't like. Similarly, in the month before the annual performance evaluations, ambitious (but unscrupulous) officers might be tempted to send a string of anonymous commendations recommending themselves for nomination as "officer of the year."

REGISTER A COMPLAINT WITH THE FEDERAL BUREAU OF INVESTIGATION

For matters related to alleged civil rights violations, you can register a complaint with any local Federal Bureau of Investigation (FBI) office by telephoning, writing, going in person, or contacting the U.S. attorney in your district. Additionally, citizens may send a written complaint to this address:

> Criminal Section
> Civil Rights Division
> U.S. Department of Justice
> P.O. Box 66018
> Washington, DC 20035-6018

Among its many duties, the Federal Bureau of Investigation is responsible for investigating certain types of inappropriate behaviors by law enforcement and other personnel. For example, Color of Law and Police Misconduct cases, which fall under its purview, involve matters in which someone (at the local, state, or federal level) misuses powers assigned by the government. Off-duty actions may also be covered here if someone has asserted her official status in some way. Incidentally, these matters do not apply only to law enforcement officers; other public officials, including judges and prosecutors, are covered as well.

For law enforcement officers, the types of misconduct the FBI can investigate include excessive use of force, sexual assault, intentional false arrest, and intentional fabrication of evidence that resulted in a loss of liberty to another person. According to the FBI, it receives approximately 8,000 to 10,000 complaints of Color of Law violations annually and actively investigates about 2,800. The highest percentage of those cases each year is excessive use of force by law enforcement personnel.

An interesting section of federal law (Title 42, U.S.C., § 14141) makes it unlawful for state or local law enforcement agencies to engage in a pattern or practice of conduct that deprives persons of rights protected by the Constitution or laws of the United States.

In fact; the U.S. Department of Justice can seek civil remedies if it finds that law enforcement agencies have policies or practices that foster a pattern of misconduct by employees.

Keep in mind that actions in cases under this section are taken against an agency and not against individual officers. From an organizational point of view, problem behaviors might include a lack of supervision of officers' actions, officers not justifying or even reporting incidents involving a use of force, or insufficient or improper training. Departments also place themselves in peril when their citizen complaint process treats complainants as adversaries.

REGISTER A COMPLAINT WITH THE DISTRICT ATTORNEY IN THE COUNTY WHERE THE INCIDENT OCCURRED

If your complaint is criminal in nature, you may choose to register your complaint directly with the district attorney or county prosecutor in the county where the incident took place. As with other similar processes, the complaint can be made in writing, by telephone, or by appearance at the district attorney's office in person.

REGISTER A COMPLAINT WITH THE CIVILIAN-POLICE REVIEW BOARD

If the community where the incident took place has some form of a civilian oversight board or committee, you may choose to make a complaint with it. In most cases, group members will forward your complaint to the police department for investigation, but your contact with them will at least establish a formal record of your having come forward. Some police departments list the contact information for their version of the civilian-police review board on the agency Web page.

As discussed earlier, the concept of citizen oversight of policing is in a constant state of flux. Some communities that once had a review board no longer do, while other cities struggle to develop some type of system to simultaneously satisfy the needs of the police department and those of citizen groups. Many believe the fears law enforcement leaders express about citizen oversight are vastly overblown, and the model presented by Sheriff Leroy Baca in Los Angeles County, California, is a welcome breath of fresh air.

REGISTER A COMPLAINT WITH THE COMMUNITY OMBUDSPERSON

Boise, Idaho, has a new and innovative position in city government known as community ombudsman. An interesting hybrid of a city auditor and a police-citizen review board, the position was created in July 1999 with a charge to investigate complaints against Boise city police and law enforcement officers. The community ombudsman is independent of all other city departments and reports directly to the mayor and city council. In addition to investigating misconduct, the ombudsman has the mission of ensuring that police policies and procedures are consistent with the needs of the community.

The concept of a community ombudsman is interesting and holds a great deal of promise. A comprehensive Web site contains the ombudsman's annual report, a complaint and commendation form suitable for downloading, and several of his findings, which are open for public scrutiny.

REGISTER A COMPLAINT WITH THE AMERICAN CIVIL LIBERTIES UNION

The American Civil Liberties Union (ACLU) is a nonprofit, nonpartisan organization dedicated to protecting the most basic civil liberties of all Americans and extending those liberties to groups that have traditionally been denied access to them. Its mission is to ensure that the Bill of Rights—the amendments to the U.S. Constitution that guard against unwarranted government control—is preserved for each new generation. Some areas of special interest to the ACLU are criminal justice, free speech, immigrant rights, lesbian and gay rights, national security, privacy, racial equality, and religious liberty.

If you believe your rights have been violated, you may contact your local chapter of the ACLU. Affiliated chapter phone numbers are available through directory assistance or can be found on the ACLU Web page.

Register a Complaint with the Police Complaint Center

Housed at Florida State University, the Police Complaint Center (PCC) is a nonprofit organization established to assist individuals who claim to have been victimized by police misconduct. Taking the position that accountability is an essential part of the public service mission of police organizations, the PCC provides assistance with reporting complaints to appropriate enforcement agencies. While the organization takes the position that it never intends to hinder or embarrass law enforcement, it emphasizes that misconduct and failure to receive complaints by the police must be publicized to prevent recurrence.

In the fall of 1999, the PCC partnered with an investigative TV news crew in Dallas–Fort Worth, Texas; it assigned a young man to test and record police responses as he inquired about the procedures for making a complaint against a police officer (see Chapter 7). The PCC Web site lists a number of police departments nationwide that it commends for properly handling similar requests for complaint information; New Orleans, Louisiana, received a grade of B+, for example, and Glendale, California, earned an A+. Several agencies (including those in Georgetown, Texas; Melbourne, Florida; and Union City, California) were also recognized for responding professionally when sent complaints of police misconduct. As you might imagine, the PCC lists a number of other agencies that it says did not do their jobs professionally.

Complaints can be made to the Police Complaint Center in several ways:

1. From its Web page, you can download a complaint form, complete it, and then mail or fax it back.
2. You can contact the PCC by telephone at 850-894-6819, extension 15. The PCC says someone will call you back within twenty-four hours and at the approximate time you request. He or she will then take your complaint over the phone.
3. You can submit your name and address through the PCC Web page. Within five business days, the organization will send you a complaint form. If you prefer, it will fax the form to you.
4. You can fill out the online complaint form on the PCC Web site.

Contact information for the Police Complaint Center is as follows:

Police Complaint Center
4244-223 West Tennessee St.
Tallahassee, FL 32304
850-894-6819, ext. 15

www.policeabuse.com

When it receives a complaint form, the PCC files it with the internal affairs section of the agency in question and sends a copy to the U.S. Department of Justice. If the police agency does not respond within thirty days, the PCC automatically sends a follow-up letter. Since all complaints are sent via certified mail, there is a $10 charge to cover that expense.

You may also pursue other avenues of redress, including contacting elected officials (mayor, county commissioner, or alder-person) and the news media (television, radio, or print). The point is, if you feel you are a victim of police misconduct, do not let any-one discourage you from making a complaint. You have an absolute right as an American citizen to have your grievance heard, and police departments need to know of problem behaviors in their ranks. Most thoughtful law enforcement leaders would agree.

Police departments provide an important service in the community, and every citizen should be mindful of and grateful for what they do. But police officers are public servants, and in a democracy we cherish and believe in the rule of law and the consent of the governed. They work for us. Perhaps Roger Baldwin, founder of the American Civil Liberties Union, said it best: "So long as we have enough people in this country willing to fight for their rights, we'll be called a democracy."

If you feel you are a victim of police misconduct and intend to file a complaint, you will need some information. Some of it, as you will see, is easily obtainable at the scene of the incident at issue, and some can be collected later. As you go about putting together the data you will use to support your complaint, remain mindful of several things:

1. The best way to avoid any difficulty with the police—and the subsequent need to complain about misconduct—is to obey the law and behave appropriately at all times.

2. Although you may be angry and upset, remain polite and respectful, stay calm, and keep your words, body language, and emotions under control.
3. Don't argue, complain, or tell the police they are wrong while at the scene.
4. Don't tell the police at the scene that you are going to file a complaint.

IDENTIFY THE OFFICER OR OFFICERS INVOLVED

You should proceed cautiously in asking for precise information at the scene, especially if you have already indicated your intention to file a complaint. The information you receive may be inaccurate, or your request may exacerbate the situation. There are a number of ways of obtaining the identification of specific officers:

1. *Name tag.* Almost all police agencies require that uniformed officers wear some type of identifying device on the uniform shirt. Undercover officers, detectives, and certain other special units may not have a visible identifier.
2. *Name written on a citation.* If you have received some type of citation or traffic ticket, the officer should have signed it and, usually, put a badge or identifier number on it as well.
3. *Police department work records.* If you know the time and location of the incident, the identity of on-duty officers assigned to a particular area can often be obtained through an examination of time sheets, work schedules, or radio call sheet records. Private citizens are generally not given access to research these records, but it is important to know they are available.
4. *Officer identification.* If other means are not available, you may choose to ask the officer for identification. Be very careful if you decide to do so because some officers may be highly offended by your request. If you ask for identification at the scene, an officer may be suspicious of your motives.
5. *Race and gender of the officer.* Make a note of the gender and apparent racial or ethnic makeup of each officer involved in the incident. Note, also, the color of hair and approximate height and weight of each officer as nearly as you can estimate.

6. *Style or color of uniform.* Since multiple agencies may have jurisdiction in a given area, it is important to accurately identify police departments involved or at the scene. What color were the uniforms? Did any uniform features, such as shoulder patches or type of headgear, stand out?

7. *Police vehicle.* Was there a police vehicle at the scene? More than one? Identify the make and model of vehicle. Note the color scheme. Record the plate numbers, and look for any other identifying numbers or symbols on the vehicle. If vehicles from more than one agency appear to be present, note that fact as well.

IDENTIFY THE EXACT JURISDICTION AND LOCATION

To identify specific jurisdictional boundaries, it is essential that you record, as precisely as possible, the location where the incident occurred. This is important information because it will not only help pinpoint specific police agencies but also identify other resources (prosecutors, for example) who may offer additional support. Do the following:

1. If the incident occurred in a municipality, note the street name. What was the nearest intersecting street? What was the exact address?

2. If it occurred on the street, note the specific location as accurately as you can. If there were any utility poles (electric or telephone) nearby, note the identification numbers on the poles.

3. To identify specific locations in rural areas, note the name of the road or highway (such as County Road 1641 or State Road 55) and then how far you were from another permanent landmark. Following is an example: "This incident took place on the north shoulder of State Highway 181, approximately 1.8 miles east of the intersection with Hurley Road." If there were utility poles nearby, note the identification numbers on them.

4. Along every interstate highway, you can find delineators to help identify specific locations. Note and record the numbers on the delineator closest to the scene of the incident. In addition, it would be wise to locate and note the nearest exit. Following is an example: "This incident took place on the east shoulder of Interstate 91, northbound, approximately 2.7 miles south of the intersection with Roberts Highway."

Pinpoint the Time of the Incident

Knowing the time of the incident, as accurately as possible, will be important. In the process of identifying officers or units at the scene, having a notation of the exact time will allow a cross-check of work records and radio call logs.

Record Any Injuries Received

For any claim of injury, you will be asked a number of hard questions. To support your case, you should collect all records, photographs, and medical reports applicable to your case. Risk managers and insurance providers look very carefully at any claims of physical injury, so you should be prepared to provide a full and vigorous defense of your allegation. Following are guidelines to ensure you take sufficiently detailed notes:

1. Are there photographs of your injury? Who took them? Where are the photos and negatives? When (exact time and date) were the photographs taken?
2. Did you seek medical treatment for your injury? When (time and date) were you treated? Where were you treated? What is the name of the physician? Do you have the records of your treatment? What was the diagnosis?
3. How did you receive the injury you are claiming? Was any police equipment used to inflict the injury? What kind of equipment? Handgun? Shoulder weapon? Baton? Other?

Note Supervisory Response and Follow-Up

If you spoke to a supervisor at the time and location where the incident took place, make a note of his name and a synopsis of the conversation you had. If you asked to speak with a supervisor and none was summoned, note that as well. If a supervisor came to the scene but did not talk with you or do anything to resolve the situation, be sure to keep notes on that fact.

When it comes to identifying and resolving conflicts between members of the public and law enforcement officers, the on-the-street patrol supervisor provides an essential link from the citizen to the police department as a whole. The first-line supervisor has a responsibility to oversee the work of her subordinates; if she falls short in this regard, the agency can be held liable for her failure. Most professional law enforcement organizations have gone to considerable lengths to educate supervisors and impress on them the critical nature of their roles in providing customer service and handling citizen complaints. As a result, when the well-trained first-line supervisor intercedes and takes corrective action where necessary, she knows she is protecting not only herself but also the citizen, the department, and other police officers.

As mentioned previously, citizens have more than a simple *right* to report inappropriate behavior by a police officer; they have an *obligation* to do so. Removing problem officers from a police department is an important task, but it cannot be accomplished by the leaders of any organization working in a vacuum. They need the support of, and input from, members of the community with a genuine interest in making things better.

DISCUSSION QUESTIONS

1. What factors would potentially discourage a citizen from making a complaint against a police officer?
2. If a citizen is dissatisfied with the actions of a police officer, why might he choose to register his complaint with an outside organization instead of the police department where the officer is employed?
3. In making a complaint against the police, why is it important to obtain and record as much identifying information as possible about the incident?
4. What should be the role of police unions or associations when it comes to defending officers accused of wrongdoing? Should the gravity of any charges against an officer make a difference?

chapter 10

BRIDGING THE GAP
BETWEEN CITIZENS
AND POLICE

To the Citizen: Before reading this chapter, think of some strategies that might help ease tensions and reduce misunderstanding between citizens and police. Are any programs under way in your community or elsewhere? How successful have they been? Why? And on a personal level, what can you do individually to foster better and more cooperative relationships with the law enforcement community?

To the Police Officer: As you read this chapter, consider any changes in policing styles you may have experienced over the course of your career. Are you and other officers expected to do your jobs differently today than you were just a few years ago? If so, what has brought about changes? Do programs such as community-oriented policing and "Courtesy, Professionalism, and Respect" (CPR) make the job of a police officer easier or harder? How do they impact the effectiveness or efficiency of law enforcement?

If the relationship between citizens and police is sometimes strained, help may be on the horizon. Many forward-looking, progressive law enforcement leaders are embracing innovative programs designed to turn things around, and the effects are being felt in a number of communities. Yes, some of these initiatives have been forced on them as a result of lawsuits or through political pressure, but most often police departments have changed their thinking on these issues simply because it makes good sense to do so.

Change takes place slowly in the law enforcement profession. The true mission of policing, after all, is to protect the status quo, not to agitate for change. Many police leaders take this charge very seriously, and their organizations often reflect their thinking. The New York State Police, for example, is a proud organization with a long and glorious history. Its informal motto, though, is "75 years of history . . . unimpeded by progress!"

Much to the chagrin of the remaining old-school police leaders still out there, the days of the walking post officer ringing the Gamewell box on the corner every hour and watching for the light to come on if the sergeant needed him are gone. Today, thoughtful law enforcement managers know that communities are policed most effectively when the citizens who live there are involved. And even in times of diminished resources, these leaders also know that time and money spent training officers and preparing them to work in concert with citizens are essential and worthy investments.

COMMUNITY POLICING

Community policing, more than any other single initiative, reflects the importance of the citizen to the efforts of law enforcement. Police actions, by themselves, rarely have a cause-and-effect relationship on crime, and efficient agencies are often no more effective than inefficient agencies in reducing crime. The key in community policing is to bring community resources to bear in a collaborative effort to control crime. According to Bob Trojanowicz et al. (1994), community policing is "a philosophy of full-service, personalized policing where the same officer patrols and works in the same area on a permanent basis, from a decentralized place, working in a proactive partnership with citizens to identify and solve problems."

The U.S. Department of Justice Community Oriented Policing Service (COPS) says community policing is most effective when a law enforcement agency and law-abiding citizens work together to arrest offenders, prevent crime, solve ongoing problems, and improve the overall quality of life. Often mischaracterized as "soft on crime," community policing is actually proactive law enforcement, and those who would harm others or steal their property find themselves under arrest. But, most important, instead of concentrating solely on enforcement, community policing officers work in concert with citizens to discover and implement strategies to improve the overall quality of life in neighborhoods.

Some of the most effective efforts are those that require little more than imagination and initiative. At a neighborhood gas station where suspected gang members would loiter at night in a dark alley, officers convinced the owner to put up more lights. Problem solved. When an officer on a visit to a senior citizens' center learned of residents' concerns about drug activity on a nearby corner, he immediately directed a high-enforcement effort to the area and gave the seniors a direct number to contact him if need be. The problem disappeared. Officers in another area removed a bank of outdoor pay phones where gang members hung around, and they solved a parking problem by convincing local school officials to allow parking in a school lot on weekends and when school was out. The quality of life in the neighborhood improved as a result.

As of July 2000, approximately 87 percent of the United States was served by a department that practices community policing. And according to COPS, as community police officers have reduced crime and fear and restored a sense of order, they have also been instrumental in rebuilding the bond between citizens and the government. Frontline officers who interact with citizens on a daily basis have a unique opportunity to demonstrate the importance of citizen involvement in the community. As public servants, these officers also come to understand that their authority and effectiveness are linked directly to the support they receive from citizens. At the end of the day, community policing is democracy at its very best.

COURTESY, PROFESSIONALISM, AND RESPECT

In 1997 the New York City Police Department (NYPD) implemented a department-wide program designed to improve relations between police officers and citizens. The effects of this program, known as Courtesy, Professionalism, and Respect (CPR), have been felt across the organization, but they have been particularly noticeable in two precincts where the commanders took an active and personal interest in having the program succeed. According to *Law Enforcement News* ("NYPD Bosses Have Their Cake and Eat It," July/August 1999), citizen complaints against police officers in the 42nd and 44th Precincts in the South Bronx dropped 67 per-cent between 1996 and 1999; crime rates dropped during the same period as well. For example, a total of 134 murders were commit-ted in these two precincts in 1990; by 1998, that number had dropped to 24.

To make the CPR program work effectively, the two com-manders installed training sergeants to ensure that their message of respectful policing was being heard by all and reinforced it by making CPR a central element in roll call and unit training programs. They also made sure that young officers with attitude problems were paired up with more experienced and mature officers. But their most impressive success has been in simultane-ously lowering both crime rates and citizen complaints. As Captain Tom King, commanding officer of the 42nd Precinct, explains, "The thought always was that if you make a lot of arrests, you're gonna get complaints. But we're out to deliver the whole package—safe streets and people who respect us because we respect them. Why accept less?" (*Law Enforcement News*, July/August 1999, p. 5).

Even today many police station houses in New York City are constructed in a design reminiscent of something from the nine-teenth century. There is typically a high desk in the reception room similar to a judge's bench in a courtroom. In front of the desk is a metal bar that citizens may approach, and in back of the desk stands the desk officer, usually a sergeant or lieutenant. In these settings, when citizens come in to transact business, the desk officer peers down at them from on high. As part of the move to reduce complaints against the police, even the architecture in the 44th Precinct was changed (the high desk and bar were removed) to better fit the culture and demonstrate responsive-ness to community concerns.

CULTURAL DIVERSITY TRAINING

The racial, ethnic, and gender composition of American society is changing at an unprecedented rate, and, according to *Workforce 2020* (Judy and D'Amico, 1997), it will continue to do so. Given the complexities of law enforcement work, therefore, it is easy to see the importance of diversity training and cross-cultural communi-cation skills to police officers. Incidentally, since the U.S. Depart-ment of Justice reports that American law enforcement employees (overall) are approximately 90 percent male and 80 percent white, cultural diversity and understanding are workplace issues as well. Fortunately, a number of high-quality training programs are available to organizations choosing to take advantage of them.

One department electing to do so is Oak Park, Illinois, an integrated town bordering the impoverished West Side of Chicago. When the police chief began receiving complaints of racially motivated traffic stops in his community, he took prompt and assertive action to change the culture of his 118-member agency. According to an article by Shipler in the *New York Times* (March 18, 1999), he began by sending all his officers through a cultural diversity training program. He then moved his department fully into the community policing model and transformed it from an agency that was overwhelmingly white into one with twenty-three black and five Hispanic members.

To prevent anyone from posting racist or sexist caricatures on the walls at police headquarters, the chief instituted a policy prohibiting the display of anything except official memoranda. To make the point even more firmly, he suspended an officer who used a racial epithet on the phone and fired another for scrawling racist graffiti in the bathroom. The chief of police in Oak Park believes in leading by example and that holding the line on small infractions will head off larger ones. He also takes the position that spending the time and money on quality training for his people will pay off for both the department and the community.

CITIZEN POLICE ACADEMIES

A fairly recent innovation, citizen police academies (CPAs) have proved to be highly effective in using education to foster better communication between citizens and the police. Everyone benefits when citizens understand the role and function of their police department, and these programs have given CPA graduates insights into how police officers perform their duties and how the department serves the community. Graduates can then share their knowledge and experiences with the community as opportunities arise.

Offered free of charge, classes are generally open to any interested citizen residing in the jurisdiction of the department offering a CPA, with only a few restrictions. Most agencies have minimum age requirements (somewhere between eighteen and twenty-one) for example, and exclude persons with criminal backgrounds. Some

CPAs restrict participation to citizens with no prior felony convictions, whereas others specify that participants have no criminal record other than traffic violations. Participants attend a series of weekly classes taught by police instructors on a range of police-related topics. Some CPAs provide opportunities for ride-alongs with a police officer, a tour of the local jail facility, or even hands-on experience with firearms or defensive tactics training.

As it is with community policing, citizen participation in a CPA improves communication with law enforcement and allows the police department to keep channels of input and support open throughout the community. One CPA graduate expressed her feelings about the experience this way: "I'm proud to be a part of this Citizen Academy and recommend it highly to all who really want to know the Lexington-Fayette Urban County Police, who protect and serve. They are concerned about the welfare of our community." Another participant added, "The Citizen Police Academy has been one of the greatest experiences of my seventy-nine years of life. Everyone should have this privilege of learning and seeing the other side of everything. It's great."

RECRUITING AND HIRING FROM THE COMMUNITY

In the continuing effort to improve relationships with and services to the communities they are sworn to protect, police departments have for many years undertaken and supported minority recruitment programs. In addition, some organizations, even in the face of typically strong union opposition, have called for residency requirements for police officers. And although both initiatives have, over time, met with mixed results, most objective observers agree that it is important to hire officers who have a stake in the community and who share a bond of understanding with the citizens they will be serving.

Some three weeks after the Amadou Diallo incident in February 1999, the New York City Police Department began a massive recruitment campaign in an effort to attract more city residents to the force. Recognizing the importance of changing the face of a department that was roughly 68 percent white in a city that was roughly 38 percent white, the mayor and police commissioner pushed for a residency requirement as well. As a result, persons seeking to be hired as NYPD police officers now must reside in one of the five New York City boroughs or one of six nearby counties.

Sometimes, despite the best efforts of the department, minority recruitment efforts fail. The New Jersey State Police, for example, relied on an extensive and well-advertised campaign to bring more blacks, women, and Latinos into the force, but it fell well short of expectations. In the new recruit class that began in September 2000, only 15 out of 105 cadets were black or Latino and only 1 was a woman. According to the superintendent of the New Jersey State Police (Kocieniewski, *New York Times*, August 23, 2000), the new class would do little to change the makeup of his organization of 2,800 members, in which 14 percent are members of minority groups and 3 percent are women.

But minority recruitment is not a panacea for the tensions between the police and the community. According to James Hill (2000), some African Americans say that although white police officers are at times abusive and insensitive, black officers sometimes seem even worse. Black officers counter by pointing out that they are in the difficult position of straddling the line between personal and professional allegiance while dealing with people of their own race. "The statement I hear all the time is 'I would expect that from a white officer, not from a brother,' " says a black ten-year veteran Chicago cop. "Like, what, I'm supposed to overlook your crime because we are both black?"

The U.S. Department of Justice Community Oriented Policing Service takes something of a middle-ground approach to the issue of recruiting; it suggests that departments should hire in the "spirit of service" rather than in the "spirit of adventure." In other words, it believes there is a link between the manner in which officers view and treat citizens in their own neighborhood and the way those citizens perceive and support their police departments. According to COPS, police officers hired in the spirit of service and trained in community policing will be instrumental to the transformation of policing in America.

SEEKING, HIRING, AND PROMOTING PEOPLE OF GOOD CHARACTER

When it comes to the suggestion that law enforcement agencies should actively recruit and then employ only personnel of integrity and good character, the phrase that instantly springs to mind is "easier said than done." Or, as one cynical police background investigator put it, "Recruiting today is like panning for gold; you've got to sift through lots of dirt before you find that one shining nugget!"

On the other hand, there is truth in the old motto that "Birth is easier than resurrection." In other words, it is far easier (and safer) to do the necessary hard work screening candidates on the front end of a career than trying (often unsuccessfully) to remove a problem officer from the ranks once he has passed his probationary period and been awarded tenure. The same holds true, by the way, when it comes to the manner in which agencies promote personnel to higher ranks or positions of trust. Fortunately, there are a number of strategies available for making ethics a central issue in the selection and screening process, both for new recruits who seek employment and for tenured officers who are eligible for advancement or special assignment.

For agencies interested in making the discussion and examination of ethics an important ingredient in the hiring or promotion process, there are several excellent ways of doing so:

1. Have the candidate read key phrases in the law enforcement code of ethics and then *explain their meaning*. What, for example, does it mean to "keep my private life unsullied"? It is easy to read a phrase and provide an explanation for what individual words mean, but this question requires far more: It requires the respondent to relate certain themes to life and work in the law enforcement profession.

2. As was done with the code of ethics, ask the candidate to read the law enforcement oath of honor and then *define the key terms* it embodies.

3. Most law enforcement agencies have crafted a values or mission statement that presumes to outline the philosophy of the organization and the values for which it stands. Hand a copy of the values or mission statement to the candidate, ask her to read it, and then have her *explain what it means*.

4. Provide the candidate with a scenario outlining a law enforcement situation (either fictional or true) with ethical dimensions. First, require him to identify the ethical issues inherent in the scenario; second, have him relate the steps he would take to resolve the situation.

5. Ask the employment candidate to list and define the character issues associated with work in a law enforcement environment.

For officers seeking promotion or assignment, require them to identify and then explain the ethics issues associated with the position they are seeking. For example, what ethics issues might be associated with assignment to the tactical unit or SWAT team? If someone requests to work in an undercover drug assignment, what does she imagine the ethical challenges will be?

END RACIAL PROFILING ACT OF 2001

With its predecessor, the Traffic Stops Statistics Study Act of 1999, tied up in committee, the End Racial Profiling Act of 2001 was introduced with a simple yet powerful mechanism for gaining cooperation and participation from police departments across the United States: It links the receipt of federal funds to the collection of traffic stop data. Introduced in June 2001, the bill provides victims of racially motivated police stops with the ability to sue police agencies that have violated their rights. In addition, it allows the attorney general to mandate the collection of traffic enforcement and search statistics, and it requires that the data be analyzed and then reported. In support of that effort, the legislation also provides grant funds for data collection and associated management programs.

In response to growing pressure, some police departments have already begun to make changes. In 2001, Washington State Patrol, for example, stopped providing awards and special recognition to officers who made numerous drug arrests, fearful that such commendations might have been causing and reinforcing problem behaviors associated with traffic stops.

In a similar move, the California Highway Patrol (CHP), in February 2003, announced a ban on consent searches and restrictions on drug-related pretext stops by their officers. As part of an effort to reinforce an organizational posture opposed to racial profiling, CHP became the first law enforcement agency in the United States to prohibit officers from asking motorists for consent to search their cars or persons.

On the East Coast, the New Jersey Association of Chiefs of Police (NJACP), in March 2002, announced their support for a state supreme court ruling that police officers must have "reasonable and articulable suspicion of criminal wrongdoing prior to seeking consent to search a lawfully stopped motor vehicle."

In their endorsement of this policy, NJACP acknowledged two important points: (1) Consent searches are a legally permissible exception to the warrant requirement and an important law enforcement tool, and (2) there is a need to place limitations on the conduct of police in order to prevent overzealous officers from abusing their authority.

In the midst of the ongoing debate about the collection of traffic stop data, a number of federal and state agencies have already begun to gather statistics on their own. In August 2000, for example, the Arlington, Texas, Police Department instituted a program to *prevent* racial profiling rather than having to *react* to it down the road (Spangler, *Fort Worth Start Telegram,* 2000). According to the chief of police in Arlington, the system requires officers to enter data electronically on the race, gender, and residence of every person stopped. Initially planned for a six-month trial, the system is now permanent.

Despite the efforts of a few forward-looking agencies, much work remains to be done throughout the law enforcement profession. Consider, for example, that when the End Racial Profiling Act of 2001 was introduced, almost 90 percent of American police agencies were not collecting profile-related data on traffic stops conducted by their officers.

Police leaders opposed to the collection of traffic stop data say they are troubled about a number of issues, including fear that the information-gathering process for police officers on the street will be too time-consuming and intrusive to make the effort practical. In Arlington, though, the required data are collected with just a few coded keystrokes on a mobile digital terminal, and, for the most part, citizens do not notice any change in the way they interact with police officers.

Opponents also express concerns about the manner in which traffic stop statistics will be used once the data are collected. Shortly after the data-gathering program was instituted in Houston, for example, some officers simply stopped writing tickets in certain sections of the city. Some white Houston officers assigned to work in largely minority neighborhoods said they feared that analysis of statistics showing they stopped mostly minority citizens would somehow be used to accuse them of being racists. When this issue was brought into the open, it became obvious that traffic stop data, once collected, must be properly interpreted as well.

POLICE LEADERS WILLING TO CHAMPION ETHICALLY STRONG ORGANIZATIONS

Any move toward enhancing relationships with citizens must be undergirded by energetic, enthusiastic, and ethically sound law enforcement leadership. There are a number of things managers and supervisors can do to improve the climate in their organizations, but four particularly powerful and straightforward strategies stand out:

1. *Be a role model.* While each member of the organization should conduct herself or himself in such fashion that her or his actions will always be an impeccable demonstration of good behavior, this is a particularly important issue for those in leadership positions. And when it comes to setting an example, everyone—regardless of rank—should behave in accordance with the same set of rules and be held to the same set of standards. Police officers are excellent students of human behavior, and when someone (a leader, for example) is insincere in his attempts to set an example, cops will immediately recognize the act for what it is—an act. The most effective and memorable role models are those who consistently exhibit right behavior and strength of character as they quietly go about doing their jobs and living their lives.

2. *Provide effective ethics training.* Do you want to know which law enforcement organization will soon be embracing agency-wide ethics training? Check the newspaper headlines. Sad to say, history shows that a leader's decision to contact an ethics consultant or trainer has often been motivated by the recent (or imminent) eruption of a scandal, or a soon-to-be-released unfavorable investigative report. Like the discussion of role modeling, ethics training—in order to be effective—must be provided routinely, not in response to some recent event that caused embarrassment to the organization. Effective ethics training must also do the following:

    a. Be presented by competent, motivated, and well-prepared faculty. Simply assigning someone to stand in front of a group of officers and read the rules, regulations, and ethics policy will be a waste of everyone's time.

b. Provide proven and easily understood decision-making tools and demonstrate their utility. In the past, "ethics training" has often consisted of a senior officer standing in front of the group, wagging a finger, and telling everyone to "stop taking free coffee." Such programs are a waste of everyone's time.

c. Treat people as adults. Once employees are given the tools necessary to identify ethical dilemmas and make informed ethical choices, there should be an expectation that they will utilize them. Thereafter, if someone behaves unethically, he should be taken to task; actions, after all, have consequences.

d. Involve everyone in the agency. When a scandal occurs, the decision is often made to send all the line (lower-ranking) personnel to an ethics class, without requiring upper levels of the organization to participate. When this happens, it is not uncommon to hear participants openly decry the fact that the folks with the real ethical issues ("the bosses") are not in the room!

3. *Create dialogue.* Ethics training is essential, but opportunities to talk about ethics should not be limited just to those times when people are gathered in class. Ethics discussions—dialogue—should become a regular part of leadership behavior. When a staff meeting is being held to craft a new policy or even mete out discipline, for example, someone at the table should be prepared to inquire about the various ethical dimensions that may come to bear. How will employees and their families be affected? What will be the impact on the larger community? On taxpayers? On other criminal justice agencies? Should other alternatives be weighed and considered?

4. *Identify and reward ethical conduct.* Law enforcement is a profession in which practitioners have historically distinguished themselves by engaging in remarkable feats of physical courage. Organizations have developed elaborate processes for identifying, recording, and rewarding—sometimes posthumously—acts of gallantry and valor. It is essential that acts of physical bravery continue to be celebrated, but in addition, leaders must also become more adept at identifying and applauding acts of moral courage . . . and

they can be found everywhere. From the officers who take it upon themselves to collect money from others on their shift to provide food and temporary housing for a stranded family of strangers to the deputy who reaches into her own pocket to buy a coat for a poorly dressed child in the winter, the ranks of law enforcement abound with examples of generosity, caring, respect, and altruism.

RECEIPTS FOR POLICE-CITIZEN CONTACTS

When it was suggested some thirty years ago that police officers hand out forms to citizens describing why they had been stopped, the idea was dismissed as impractical because of the time and paperwork involved in the process. Today, though, anyone who has ever rented a car and returned it to an airport has seen modern technology at work. By the time you have taken your bags out of the trunk, the agent has printed out an instant receipt with all your information, and you are on your way. Why not a similar system to account for police-citizen interactions?

According to an article by Sterngold in the *New York Times* (March 21, 2000), supporters of the idea describe it as a direct response to the national concern about racial profiling and the manner in which the police select people for on-the-street interrogations. Requiring officers to provide receipts would be a way of easing tensions on the street, they say, while creating a sense of accountability and legitimacy that has been lacking. And since the police know there will be records of interactions, supporters of the idea predict there would be fewer unnecessary stops and frisks.

In the New York Police Department, officers are already required to fill out a form when they stop and frisk a citizen. But since these reports go only to their immediate supervisors, officers may submit inaccurate information or skip the task altogether. In fact, some members of the NYPD say they have known other officers who fill out the mandatory form only about one time in ten. Requiring officers to hand a receipt to a citizen on the street would presumably make officers more conscientious about record keeping and perhaps their behavior as well.

When the idea of giving receipts to citizens came up for discussion in a class of in-service police officers, one crusty old street cop listened quietly to the debate. Eventually he spoke, making a suggestion everyone else in the room instantly supported. "There is one other benefit to these receipts," he noted. "When some citizen gets six of them, we can let him trade them in on a toaster."

This skeptical officer aside, handing out receipts sometimes really does reap unexpected rewards for the police. During a campaign to remove illegal guns from the streets in Prince Georges County, Maryland, officers stopped as many cars as possible for minor traffic violations. After each vehicle was pulled over, officers politely explained the reason for the traffic stop and handed each motorist a letter explaining the crackdown and listing a phone number to call with any complaints. It is noteworthy that even though the police dramatically increased traffic enforcement through this effort, the number of complaints from citizens actually dropped. According to Dr. Lawrence Sherman (2000), "People respond better when they're treated as equals instead of being confronted with orders from superiors" (p. 16).

CITIZEN SELF-ARREST PROCESS

Maybe the police department at the University of Oklahoma has a point. If there is tension between citizens and the police, the solution may lie in removing or at least minimizing any contact the two groups have with each other. To that end, the university police have created what is known as the Citizen's Self-Arrest Form and placed it on their Web page (www.ou.edu/oupd/self-arr2.htm). Their philosophy is simple: (1) If you witness a crime, it is your civic duty to report the crime to the police; (2) when a crime is committed, you have the right and responsibility to make a citizen's arrest; and (3) if *you* commit a crime, it would be extremely helpful—and provide a savings of tax dollars—for you to perform a citizen's self-arrest.

The form appearing on the Oklahoma University Police Department Web page is extremely helpful and user-friendly and provides a slightly revised version of the Miranda warning you can read to yourself. Directions are included on the best way to take your own fingerprints; if you do not have a passport photo to send with the form, the instructions suggest you sketch yourself. Once you have described your crime in the space provided, the form directs you to confine yourself to your house, although allowances are made for people who might prefer to send in their self-arrest form by mail instead of by computer or fax machine. In these situations, you are permitted one trip to the mailbox. The form can be completed conveniently online if you choose to do so; you conclude the process by clicking the "Arrest Yourself Now" button.

DISCUSSION QUESTIONS

1. What changes, if any, have the events of September 11, 2001, brought about in the levels of understanding, openness, and cooperation between citizens and police?
2. What are the benefits to insisting that police officers establish residency in the communities where they work? What are the drawbacks?
3. What steps can organizations and individual officers take to help ensure the success of programs such as Courtesy, Professionalism, and Respect (CPR)?
4. How can police organizations best ensure they are recruiting, hiring, and then training officers of good character?

chapter **11**

THE NOBILITY OF POLICING

To the Citizen: As you read this chapter, think about the types of people who decide to become police officers. Where are they drawn from? How are they selected? And what makes the overwhelming majority of them go out every day and willingly endanger themselves on our behalf? Do you think police departments should change the way they recruit, screen, train, or deploy their officers? What changes would you recommend?

To the Police Officer: Why did you enter law enforcement? Before you read this chapter, reflect for a few moments on the reasons you were drawn to the field of policing in the first place. Are you still motivated by these same factors? If not, has the change been in a positive or a negative direction? As a core value, do police officers define *loyalty* differently than members of other professions do Why? What about *courage*? Is it harder to show physical courage or moral courage? Why?

Twenty-five years ago, the young philosophy professor had a sure-fire technique for stimulating discussion in his college ethics classes. He would simply ask the group to consider this question: "For you, what people, issues, or principles are important enough that you might consider sacrificing your life for them?" In his experience, the ensuing debate would include a range of responses from the young students, including those who could envision going to war and dying in defense of liberty, others who would lay down their lives for family, and those few who said they could foresee no circumstance under which they would give up their lives on behalf of a cause or another person.

That young professor is now twenty-five years older and chair of the philosophy department at a small Midwestern university. He still teaches ethics classes at his college but says there are two reasons why he no longer asks his students the "sacrifice" question: (1) his personal feelings of disappointment at the current crop of students who seem unable to even imagine the possibility of sacrifice for any reason whatsoever, and (2) his concern that the young students will think him demented for having the temerity to ask such a ridiculous question.

Lately, though, the professor has experienced a renewal of his faith in humanity's ability to wrestle with value-laden issues and to do so in a real-world environment. The professor, you see, has begun teaching and leading ethics dialogues with law enforcement in-service classes. As a result, he is learning something that police officers have always known: Law enforcement is a truly noble profession. After all, very few others in society willingly go out every day and put themselves in harm's way—often on behalf of total strangers—in the way police officers do. And as the college professor has come to understand, cops, better than most people, know what it means to sacrifice. Every year, they (and we) stand far too often in broken-hearted witness as law enforcement officers demonstrate—at the cost of their lives—the true meaning of altruism.

GROWING INTO THE LAW ENFORCEMENT PROFESSION

Work in the field of law enforcement provides boundless opportunity to do good, but not every police officer enters the field for exactly the same reason. Most, it may be assumed, are attracted to a career in law enforcement because they see it as a way to make the community a safer, better place. Others are attracted by the opportunity for a secure job with relatively good benefits. And a few, unfortunately, seek to become cops because of the power that accompanies the position. In this environment of varied employee backgrounds and motivations, then, can a law enforcement leader reasonably expect every officer to understand and support the values of the department in exactly the same way?

The problem police departments face in this regard is similar to the situations of a number of other organizations, including the U.S. military. In the U.S. Marine Corps, for example, commanders have struggled with the basic question of whether it is ever possible to impart something like ethics to young adults whose belief systems are already fairly well formed before they are sworn in. In a similar vein, many law enforcement leaders have long questioned the feasibility of trying to teach someone the parameters of acceptable behavior when he or she may not have learned and lived them before joining the agency. According to General C. C. Krulak, former commandant of the U.S. Marine Corps, a solution to this dilemma may be found in the way organizations outline their expectations for employees (*USA Today*, August 11, 1998, p. 8A):

> We are not born with character. It is developed by the experiences and decisions that guide our lives. Each individual creates, develops and nurtures his or her own character. Being a man or woman of character is not an easy task. It requires tough decisions, many of which put you at odds with the more commonly accepted social mores of the times.
>
> Marines are called upon to make ethical, life-and-death choices in the execution of their responsibilities. It is the nature of our duty. That is not the case for someone in the business sector, and arguments that advocate like standards are baseless. We cannot anticipate and train Marines for each situation they may [face;] therefore, all Marines must possess a moral consistency to serve as a compass guiding them in their integrity, honor, courage and commitment.
>
> Making the right ethical choices must become a habit. Decisions cannot be situational, based on others' actions or dependent upon [who] is watching. We must establish standards by which we expect Marines to live. When those standards are compromised, it is imperative we have the tools necessary to hold those accountable who are found lacking.

Krulak is talking about the overriding importance of organizational values that, once defined, will mark the standard to which every person in the organization will be held. Then, he says, it makes no difference how an individual young recruit may have been brought up; when he joins the Marine Corps, he will never have a doubt about what the organization stands for or the values he will be expected to emulate and support while employed there.

Police departments can use exactly the same approach, and many have done so. A number of forward-looking leaders have led the charge to develop effective mission statements, provide universal ethics training, and foster a shift toward values-based leadership. Recruitment remains an area of concern from the standpoint of values, but this is not a new phenomenon. As far back as the 1930s, law enforcement leaders publicly lamented the quality of men (they were all men at the time) entering police work, prompting August Vollmer to suggest that a successful police recruit would need the following:

> [T]he wisdom of Solomon, the courage of David, the strength of Samson, the patience of Job, and leadership of Moses; the kindness of the Good Samaritan, the strategy of Alexander, the faith of Daniel, the diplomacy of Lincoln, the tolerance of the Carpenter of Nazareth, and finally, an intimate knowledge of every branch of the natural, biological and social sciences. If he had all these, he might be a good policeman. (Vollmer, 1936, p. 222)

It would be difficult to hold police officers (or anyone else, for that matter) to Vollmer's standards. There are, however, a number of values and professional attributes that accurately define both the practice and the practitioners of law enforcement. As you peruse the sections that follow, consider this: The attributes (loyalty, honesty, integrity, respect, and courage) define the heart of what the police profession is all about in a democracy. At the same time, they represent, as we shall see, areas of considerable personal and professional conflict for those we commission to stand guard on our behalf.

LOYALTY

In the law enforcement community, loyalty can be both a blessing and a curse. It is a blessing when a police officer calls for a backup out on the street and other officers immediately and without question come to her aid. And speaking from personal experience, when a cop is down on the pavement wrestling with someone he is trying to take into custody, there is no sound sweeter to his ears than that of the sirens on a squadron of approaching police vehicles. From that standpoint, the bond of loyalty is a highly valued commodity.

Sometimes, though, loyalty among police officers can be a curse. When cops cover up for one of their peers who has behaved inappropriately, for example, it is not loyalty but rather blind loyalty. And there is a dramatic difference between the two. Fortunately, most police officers have come to understand the distinction, as well as the tremendous personal and professional costs that derive from misguided loyalty.

Confusion about the notion of loyalty is, of course, not confined solely to the law enforcement profession, as evidenced by an academic cheating scandal that erupted in the early 1990s at the U.S. Naval Academy. Asked to comment on how a service academy with an honor code and a proud reputation for trust and integrity could be embroiled in such a conflict, Colonel Michael W. Hagee, U.S. Marines, said:

> The loyalty that would cause an individual to jump on a hand grenade and save other lives is good. But to venerate loyalty at all costs, as did those students who refused to turn in their classmates for cheating, ignored a more important truth: honesty. (*New York Times*, April 3, 1994, p. 15)

Using a household pet metaphor to differentiate the two forms of loyalty, Michael Josephson, founder and president of the Josephson Institute for Ethics, uses the example of dogs (which are loyal to a person) and cats (which are loyal to a house). A "dog loyal" person, according to Josephson, would not hesitate to tell someone "I'm with you until the bitter end . . . and we'll go down the tubes together!" A "cat loyal" individual, on the other hand, would express herself in this way: "I'm loyal to you, but you need to understand that there are other loyalty relationships in my life as well. For example, I'm loyal to the community, to the department, to the Constitution of the United States. At a visceral level, I'm loyal to my family."

One of the many positive benefits of a changing workforce, especially in the police community, is the increasing willingness of the new worker to ask the question "Why?" In other words, young officers are less willing to mindlessly go along with old traditions and, for a variety of reasons, look at the issue of loyalty differently than some of their older peers. The "why" question has special meaning when it comes to the issue of covering for another cop, and although it is never voiced in exactly this way, what it comes down to is the following question: "Why should I be expected to lose my job and possibly go to jail simply because that other cop did something stupid?"

If a police officer is asked to contemplate and then write down the things that are truly important in life, the list might look something like this:

1. Family
2. Good name or reputation
3. Job and career
4. Hobbies and outside interests (especially as they might lead toward life or a job after retirement)
5. Police patrol partner and other police officers

Police officers tend to be very family-oriented, and most place the family at the top of any list of their values. It is interesting, then, to consider the lengths to which some cops will go to cover up for another officer and the risks they are willing to endure in the process. Take, for example, the issue of the off-duty cop stopped for driving while intoxicated. Although far less common today than in the past, some officers say they would always take a cop home under these circumstances; they maintain that to do so is an expression of loyalty. What they overlook, of course, is that when they take that drunk cop home, they have chosen to elevate number five on their list of important things in life to the very top and placed numbers one through four at risk.

In the twenty-first century, drunk driving is a politically sensitive and highly emotional issue. If it is proved, then, that a police officer failed to enforce the law vigorously and equally, public opinion will be negative, the police department will investigate, and disciplinary action will likely result. If the cover-up results in a suspension without pay, the officer's family will suffer (loss of income), his reputation and good name will be damaged (questions about his trustworthiness both inside and outside the agency), his job and career will be negatively impacted (limits on promotions or transfers because of character concerns), and the retirement job prospects he had been working toward through his hobbies and outside interests will be harmed (concerns about hiring someone who had been disciplined for failing to do his job as the law dictated).

In a classroom filled with officers from a number of different police departments, it is both interesting and instructive to ask two simple questions: (1) How many of you come from a police department in which an officer has died in the line of duty over the past year? and (2) How many of you come from a police department in which an officer has lost his job for behaving unethically in the line of duty over the past year? Thankfully, very few hands go up in answer to the first question. Not surprisingly, the majority in the room raise their hands in response to the second. In other words, almost every officer knows of another cop who has been fired because of misbehavior, and many of those dismissals are linked directly to an inability to distinguish between loyalty and blind loyalty.

HONESTY

Among the multitude of lawyer jokes making the rounds is the one starting with the question, "How can you tell when a lawyer is lying?" The correct answer, of course, is, "Any time his lips are moving." Police officers laugh knowingly when they hear that punch line, but if they are wise, they quickly change the subject. The last thing cops want to do in any discussion of honesty, after all, is to bring attention to themselves. In defense of law enforcement officers, they very seldom lie. On the other hand, they frequently practice the art of deception.

Let's face it: Trying to do the job of law enforcement would be extraordinarily difficult—if not impossible—without the use of deception. Can you imagine an officer trying to conduct drug buys as part of a narcotics investigation without disguising his appearance and motivation? How effective do you think a hostage negotiator would be if she couldn't use some trickery in the process? Even the U.S. Supreme Court permits police officers to use deception, within certain boundaries, in their interviews of suspects. The difficulty for a police officer testifying in a criminal case, of course, comes in having to explain that although he used deception (lied) to capture the defendant, he is now telling the truth while testifying under oath.

Most law enforcement practitioners are honest, and they recognize that deception is both a powerful and dangerous tool. Misused, it can tarnish much of the good the police are trying to accomplish. Richard Dunn (1996), an inspector with the Illinois State Police, suggests that to prevent the misuse of deception, officers should always consult with a supervisor before using duplicity to accomplish a task. If no viable option other than deception exists, then once the job is completed, the police should consciously distance themselves from the inherently dangerous world of using duplicitous behavior. If they fail to do so, Dunn says, the police run the very real risk of being tainted by the tension between their purpose and their ploys.

INTEGRITY

Saddam Hussein is a man of integrity. Strange and potentially offensive as that might sound, it is true because a person of integrity is one who lives in accordance with his or her values at all times. Most of us might not agree with the values Hussein has chosen to cling to, but we must admit that he has remained true to them. The late Mother Teresa, of course, was also a person of integrity, and from what we know of her, she—in stark contrast to Hussein—lived her life true to a very positive and uplifting set of values. Very often, police officers, in both their personal and professional lives, find themselves looked upon as role models for others in society. And generally speaking, they prove themselves worthy of that mantle. (And to their immense credit, police officers most often come down very strongly on the Mother Teresa side of the scale.)

The notion of integrity suggests an adherence to a set of values at all times. Early in their careers, cops learn to live with the fact that their behavior will be open to scrutiny whether they are on or off duty. For example, when the cop's neighbors have a couple of beers at a cookout, they are just relaxing; when the cop does the same things at the same party, though, people will ask him pointed questions about drinking and driving. When the guy next door forgets to renew his vehicle registration, it's an oversight; when the cop's personal car bears an expired plate, that's a violation of law. Neighbor kids who fill mailboxes with shaving cream on Halloween are just acting like kids; if one of them happens to be the cop's kid, he is a troublemaker who should have known better because he comes from a police family.

When we hire police officers, we entrust them with enormous power and authority; to complicate matters, we give them something else: autonomy. In other words, when police officers are out on patrol or otherwise doing the job we hire them to do, they generally perform their tasks away from direct one-on-one supervision. Although some law enforcement personnel abuse their positions and our trust, for the most part police agencies are populated by people who understand and adhere to the limits the law and their organizations place on them. Clearly, an unethical officer could make a false arrest, perjure himself, and send an innocent citizen to jail (the report on the Rampart scandal confirms this reality). That same officer—if he chose to do so—could brutally assault a citizen and claim it was in self-defense (the report on the Abner Louima case in New York City is a case in point).

The few well-publicized abuses aside, citizens in a democracy are free from false arrest, unlawful imprisonment, and pervasive police brutality, and that says something very important about the understanding and reverence law enforcement officers have for both the responsibilities and the limits of their positions. That police departments stand as bastions of permanence and right in a sometimes tumultuous society is a direct reflection of the integrity of the people who work in these organizations.

RESPECT

Although it is more than ten years old, the Rodney King video still touches some very deep chords in people who watch it. Some defensive tactics experts continue to see it as a clear demonstration of what can happen when insufficient force is applied. Others don't find the video particularly troublesome and take the position that we would have fewer problems if cops had more, rather than less, freedom to administer "street justice." But other interested observers take a very different position, arguing that the biggest problem with the way the Los Angeles Police treated Rodney King on that memorable night does not even appear on the video. From their point of view, the primary source of the problem on March 3, 1991, was something the police did *not* do. In their eyes, the Los Angeles Police Department (LAPD) failed to treat Rodney King with respect.

Respect does not mean, by the way, that police officers should have had any affection for Rodney King. Nor does it mean they should have endorsed his behavior or admired his lifestyle. By all accounts and appearances, Rodney King is not a very law-abiding or cooperative man. But that is a separate and distinct issue. Respect has nothing to do with the citizen (King, in this case); instead, it has everything to do with the police officer.

When members of a New York City Police Department warrant team entered the wrong premises in a housing project early one morning, they attempted to bust through the door but found it would not break down easily. In the commotion, a man sleeping in the apartment awakened, grabbed an admittedly unlicensed handgun, and fired at the door. The police, finding themselves under fire, began to shoot back. Fortunately, nobody was struck, but the suspect was taken into custody for the unlicensed weapon and made to sit naked and handcuffed in his hallway with all of his neighbors milling around. When the police decided to remove him to the precinct for further questioning, he asked permission to get dressed and they allowed him to do so—up to a point. They made him dress in his girlfriend's clothing.

Upon being released from the precinct several hours later, the man asked for a ride back to his home but was refused; he had to walk the eight blocks back to his apartment dressed in those same clothes. When the police commissioner appeared on a Sunday morning television talk show several weeks later, he was asked to comment on the way his officers had treated that citizen, particularly the fact that their refusal to give him a ride forced him to walk eight blocks dressed in women's clothing. The commissioner's response to the question was, "Oh, you mean the guy with the illegal handgun up in the Bronx." He made no mention of the clothing issue, the man's walk back to his apartment thus attired, or, most telling, the fact that his officers had entered the wrong apartment in the first place.

Most thoughtful police officers learn early in their careers that treating people respectfully can reap enormous rewards. Referring to a citizen as "sir" or "ma'am" makes perfect sense and eliminates any potentially offensive issues regarding rank, position, or pronunciation of someone's name. George Thompson, in his Verbal Judo training, argues that sometimes the word that springs easily to an officer's lips is the one that should be avoided at all costs. For example, in the heat of a confrontation, an officer may feel an impulse to refer to the other person as an _____ (fill in the blank). And although saying that word may momentarily make the officer feel good, it is very likely to make the situation worse rather than better.

Since the notion of respect obliges police officers to be mindful of and protect another person's dignity, some traffic officers have a unique way of handling traffic stops when the violator may be a parent driving with children in the backseat of the car. In cases when a citation has to be issued (and when safety permits), the parent-driver may be given the opportunity to step out of the vehicle where the summons can be handed over and explained out of the sight and hearing of the children. That way, free from the potential for humiliation and embarrassment, the parent can tell the children whatever he or she likes about the interaction with the police officer.

Respect also means a willingness to apologize. When an officer or a police agency makes an honest mistake (entering the wrong premises, stopping the wrong car, or handcuffing the wrong person, for example), there is genuine merit in acknowledging the error and offering a sincere apology. To use an example from the political realm, many people regret that President Bill Clinton, toward the end of the 1990s, did not have the fortitude (or respect for American citizens) to stand up and publicly proclaim "I'm a flawed individual who has made some serious mistakes. I apologize and will work as hard as I can to avoid making those same errors in the future."

COURAGE

The profession of law enforcement, unlike most other occupations, regularly places practitioners in situations in which they are called on to display extraordinary physical courage. From the Special Weapons and Tactics (SWAT) team preparing to enter a building where someone is barricaded and armed to the solo traffic officer stopping a speeder without knowing what may confront her next, the very real presence of physical danger permeates the world of the street officer. To acknowledge and applaud the brave men and women who work there, most law enforcement organizations conduct an annual awards ceremony at which life-saving, valor, heroism, and similar acts of selfless courage are commended. In some cases, unfortunately, that recognition must be awarded posthumously.

In addition to physical courage, the field of law enforcement is rife with examples of practitioners exhibiting strong moral courage as well. Following are some examples:

- Billings, Montana, Police Chief Wayne Inman led an effort to combat anti-Semitism in his community in 1994. Hate groups in the Northwest had vandalized a number of Jewish homes and businesses, so Inman asked the city newspaper to print a full-page picture of a menorah (the Jewish religious candelabra). That way, every home in Billings could display a menorah in the window and the vandals would not be able to distinguish between the Christian homes and the Jewish homes.

- When Charles Moose was chief of police in Portland, Oregon, he announced that his agency was going to take back the city block by block. To give his officers an idea of what he meant, he immediately moved his family into the King neighborhood (a high-crime area in Portland). Moose showed by his actions that he is a chief who not only talks the talk but also walks the walk. He is currently police chief in Montgomery County, Maryland.

- As the Mollen Commission was concluding hearings on the corruption scandal in the New York City Police Department in 1993, NYPD Detective Sergeant Joe Trimboli testified about his six-year effort to capture the corrupt cop at the center of that scandal and the roadblocks put in his way by higher-ups in the department. He also described in painful detail the treatment he received from other police officers as a result of his speaking out publicly. At the end of his testimony, Trimboli resigned from the NYPD.

Law enforcement leaders absolutely must continue to seek out and identify officers who show bravery and engage in acts of physical courage. As they do so, though, they must aggressively seek opportunities to reward officers who distinguish themselves through acts of moral courage as well. The term *reward* is used here rather loosely in the context of moral courage because many who have considered becoming whistle-blowers would argue that they do not want any visible or tangible reward for their efforts. Instead, they would prefer the simple assurance that if they were to step forward, the organization would protect them.

In the movie *A Few Good Men*, Jack Nicholson is perfectly cast in the role of Nathan Jessep, a crusty Marine Corps colonel and commandant of a frontline unit of troops tasked with defending the U.S. military base at Guantánamo, Cuba, from enemy incursion. Movie fans will recall the classic courtroom scene in which Jessep finds himself in the uncomfortable position of having to answer questions from Daniel Kaffee, a brash Navy lieutenant and lawyer (played by Tom Cruise). As Kaffee inquires into the circumstances surrounding the death of a young Marine named Santiago, the tension increases. Finally, outraged that an impertinent young naval officer would have the audacity to question his actions and those of his men, Jessep erupts in absolute fury:

> Son, we live in a world that has walls. And those walls have to be guarded by men with guns. Who's gonna do it? You? You, Lieutenant Weinberg? I have a greater responsibility than you can possibly fathom. You weep for Santiago and you curse the Marines. You have that luxury. You have the luxury of not knowing what I know: That Santiago's death, while tragic, probably saved lives. And my existence, while grotesque and incomprehensible to you, saves lives.
>
> You don't want the truth. Because deep down, in places you don't talk about at parties, you want me on that wall. You need me there. We use words like honor, code, loyalty . . . we use these words as the backbone to a life spent defending something. You use 'em as a punch line.
>
> I have neither the time nor the inclination to explain myself to a man who rises and sleeps under the blanket of the very freedom I provide, then questions the manner in which I provide it. I'd prefer you just said thank you and went on your way. Otherwise, I suggest you pick up a weapon and stand a post. Either way, I don't give a damn what you think you're entitled to. (reprinted with permission)

Leaving Hollywood and entering the real world of criminal justice, Colonel Jessep could be offering a stirring defense for the way some police officers see themselves and their mission. But law enforcement administrators are not Marine Corps base commanders, police officers are not combat troops on a hostile front line, and citizens are not the enemy. With that in mind, if there is to be an easing of tension between the police and the public, it will not come as a result of increased pressure for arrests, zero tolerance efforts, and militarization. Instead, it will emerge from openness, frank communication, and a willingness to listen on both sides of the divide.

As a young boy, I grew up along the banks of the Hudson River in the small village of Ossining, New York. One of my favorite pastimes was to go down along the river where the railroad tracks were located and watch the seemingly endless parade of passenger and freight trains traveling north out of New York City. To a youngster, watching those trains pass by was both exciting and adventurous.

Today, people involved in the struggle to improve the state of police-community relations are in a situation similar to mine as I stood mesmerized along the tracks many years ago, but with one notable difference. As a little boy in Ossining, New York, I was able to stand by the side and watch. People of goodwill—citizens and police alike—genuinely interested in building bridges of openness, understanding, and communication cannot do that. They have only two choices: get on the train, or stand in front of the train. Those people who will ultimately cause good things to happen in that arena cannot—and will not—stand alongside and watch that train go by.

DISCUSSION QUESTIONS

1. Beyond those listed in the chapter, what are some of the other "core values" of law enforcement? Be sure to carefully define those values.

2. If police officers admit using deception to conduct their investigations, how should they convince juries they can be trusted to tell the truth when they are testifying under oath?

3. In policing, is it easier to identify physical courage or moral courage? Which is rewarded more frequently? Why?

4. Is a police officer's job made simpler or more complex by the fact that he carries out his duties in a democratic society? Explain.

BIBLIOGRAPHY

American Civil Liberties Union. (1999, June). Racial Profiling on Our Nation's Highways [Online]. Available at: www.aclv.org/profiling/report/index.html

Arlington County (VA) Statement on Racial Profiling. (1999, December). *Subject to Debate*. Washington, D.C.: Police Executive Research Forum.

Barco, M. (2000, July 17). Dallas Police Say They Deal with Hundreds of Complaints Against Officers Each Year. *Dallas Morning News*, p. 14-A.

Blanchard, K., & Peale, N. (1996). *The Power of Ethical Management*. New York: Morrow Publishers.

Board of Inquiry, Los Angeles Police Department. (2000, March 1). Rampart Area Corruption Incident. Executive Summary. Los Angeles: Author.

Caldero, M., & Crank, J. (2000). *Police Ethics: The Corruption of Noble Cause*. Cincinnati, Ohio: Anderson Publishing.

Cannon, L. (2000, October 1). One Bad Cop. *New York Times*, p. 32.

Carlson, D. (1995, March). Looking Through the One-Way Mirror. *Texas Police Journal*, p. 11.

Chivers, C. J. (2000, September 15). Approval and Wariness in Poll on Police. *New York Times*, p. 1.

Clines, F. (1993, March 9). Police-Killers Offer Insights into Victims' Fatal Mistakes. *New York Times*, p. 21.

Connerly, W. (2000, July 2). America, Seen Through the Filter of Race. *New York Times*, p. 11.

Cooper, M. (1999, February 24). Drive to Seek More City Residents for Police Force. *New York Times*, p. 1.

Dart, G. (2001, May 11). Stopping Deadly Police Chases in Their Tracks. *Channel 2 Action News* [Online]. Available at: www.accessatlanta.com/partners/wsbtv/specialreports/highspeed2.html

Delattre, E. (1994). *Character and Cops: Ethics in Policing*, 2d ed. Washington, D.C.: AEI Press.

Dunn, R. (1996, spring). Would You Ever Lie? *Ethics Roll Call*, p. 5.

FBI Law Enforcement Bulletin, July 2000.

FBI Law Enforcement Bulletin, July 2001.

Flynn, K. (2000, April 4). 3 Officers Are Suspended in Threat to Another Officer over Arrest. *New York Times*, p. 17.

Frazier, T. (2000, August 21). A Definition of Community Policing. *U.S. Department of Justice, Community Oriented Policing Services* [Online]. Available at: www.usdoj.gov/cops/news_info/bg_definition.htm

Hagee, M. (1994, April 3). Letter to the Editor. *New York Times*, p. 15.

Hill, J. (2000, August 21). For Black Cops, Trust Hard to Gain. *Minorities Job Bank* [Online]. Available at: www.iminorities.com/african/civil/archives/blackcops0910.html

Judy, R., & D'Amico, C. (1997). *Workforce 2020: Work and Workers in the 21st Century*. Indianapolis, Indiana: Hudson Institute.

Knapp Commission. (1973). *Report on Police Corruption*. New York: G. Braziller.

Kocieniewski, D. (2000, August 23). Effort to Recruit Minorities Falls Short in Trooper Class. *New York Times*, p. 1.

The Law and You. (1999). National Association for the Advancement of Colored People. Baltimore, Maryland: National Organization of Black Law Enforcement Executives, and Allstate Insurance Company.

Letterman, D. (1984, February 9). Late Night with David Letterman. *Cool Quotes Collection* [Online]. Available at: www.sleepwalker.net/quotes.

MacDonald, H. (2003). *Are Cops Racist?* Chicago: Dee.

Milland, C. (1986, April). Why Cops Hate You. *Gallery* magazine.

Mollen Commission. (1994, July 7). *Report of the New York City Commission to Investigate Regulations of Police Corruption and the Anti-Corruption Procedures of the Police Department*. Buffalo, New York: William S. Hein & Co., Inc.

Moore, M. (1997). The Legitimization of Criminal Justice Policies and Practices. In Practices on Crime and Justice: 1996–97 Lecture Series. Washington, D.C.: National Institute of Justice.

Peterson, I. (1999, April 21). Whitman Says Troopers Used Racial Profiling. *New York Times*, p. 1.

Pinizzotto, A., Davis, E., & Miller, C. (2000, July). Officers' Perceptual Shorthand. *FBI Law Enforcement Bulletin*, pp. 1–6.

Rovella, D. (1999, November 22). Some Superinformant. *National Law Journal*, p. A-1.

Rovella, D. (2000, May 22). Cop Scandals Take Toll. *National Law Journal*, p. A-1.

Sherman, L. (2000, March 1). *Trust and Confidence in Criminal Justice*. Paper prepared for the U.S. Department of Justice.

Shipler, D. (1999, March 18). A Well-Blazed Trail for the Police. *New York Times*, p. 19.

Spangler, A. (2000, August 21). Arlington Police Plan for Traffic Stop Data. *Fort Worth Star-Telegram*, p. 1-B.

Sterngold, J. (2000, March 2). Los Angeles Police's Report Cites Vast Command Lapses. *New York Times*, p. A-14.

Stockwell, J., & Jackman, T. (2000, September 6). Prince Georges' Chief Breaks Silence on Virginia Shooting. *Washington Post*, p. A-1.

Sykes, G. (2000, summer). Ethical Crossroads: Do We Want a Militarized Police? *Ethics Roll Call*, p. 4.

Tierney, J. (2000, March 21). Keeping Tabs on the Police with Receipts. *New York Times*, p. 21.

Traffic Stops Statistics Study Act of 1999 [Online]. (1999, April 15). Available at: www.thomas.loc.gov/cgibin/query/z?c106:S.821

Trojanowicz, R., Woods, D., Harold, J., Roboussin, R., Trojanowicz, S., et al. (1994). *Community Policing: A Survey of Police Departments in the United States* [Online]. Available at: www.concentric.net/~dwoods/faq.htm

U.S. Department of Justice, Federal Bureau of Investigation, Uniform Crime Reporting Program. (2002). *Law Enforcement Officers Killed and Assaulted*, 2001. Washington, D.C.: Author.

Ventura, California, Police Department. (2000, September 9). *Policy Statement on Racial Profiling*. Ventura, California: Author.

Vollmer, A. (1936). *The Police and Modern Society*. College Park, Maryland: McGrath Publishing Co.

Walker, S. (1992, March 18). *The L.A. Incident and Policing*. Paper presented at the Southwestern Law Enforcement Institute.

Wambaugh, J. (1970). *The New Centurions*. Boston: Little, Brown & Co.

Wambaugh, J. (1975). *The Choirboys*. New York: Dell.

Weisburd, D., & Greenspan, R. (2000). Police Attitudes Toward Abuse of Authority: Findings from a National Study. *U.S. Department of Justice* [Online]. Available at: www.ncjrs.org/txtfiles1/nij/181312.txt.

Newspaper Articles

Associated Press

Houston Battles Racial Profiling. August 12, 1999, p. 1.

Judge Orders State to Turn Over Data on Police's Racial Profiling. October 24, 1999, p. 1.

Old Police Memo Details Racial Profiling. July 26, 2000, p. 1.

Dallas Morning News

LA Police Are Sued over "Code of Silence." August 26, 2000, p. 6A.

Law Enforcement News

NYPD Bosses Have Their Cake and Eat It. July/August 1999, p. 5.

Number of Slain Cops Hits All-Time Low. May 2000, p. 8.

Smoother Complaint Process Urged in KC. June 15, 2000, p. 7.

Los Angeles Times

Rampart's Rising Costs. May 12, 2000, p. B-8.

Sheriff Takes Dramatic Step for Closer Civilian Oversight. July 5, 2000, p. 26.

New York Times

To Some in the Village, Enough Already. May 3, 1998, p. 2.

St. Petersburg Times

Tarnished Police Trust. June 23, 2000, p. 2.

Wall Street Journal. September 11 Today. June 11, 2003, p. 18.

Web Pages

Evanston Citizen's Police Academy: www.evanstonpolice.com/CPA/sessions.htm

Washington Citizen's Police Academy: www.washington.xtn.net~jcpb/citizens.htm

Lexington Citizen's Police Academy: www.lexingtonpolice.lfucg.com/comserv/citacademy.html

Verbal Judo: www.JhoonRhee.com

INDEX

P

Patrolmen's Benevolent
Association, 40
Peale, Norman Vincent, 38–39
Physical condition, safety and, 45
Pitt, William, 59
Police Complaint Center
(PCC) at Florida State
University, 90
registering complaints
with, 116–118
Police culture, 29–42
passing along, 38–45
power of, 29–31
problem police officers
and, 32–33
Rodney King incident
and, 31–32
separation of society into
police and others, 33–38
"seven veils" and, 35–38
*Police Ethics: The Corruption
of Noble Cause* (Caldero
and Crank), 20
*Power of Ethical Management,
The* (Blanchard and
Peale), 38–39
Principles of professional law
enforcement, 4–12
accountability, 8–9
adherence to the oath
of office, 9–10
balanced enforcement of the
law, 4–5
objective enforcement of the
law, 10–12
openness and accessibility,
5–8
Proactive traffic enforcement, 62
Protective gear, safety of police
officers and, 47–49
Public opinion, 74
Purnick, Joyce, 40
Pursuits, high-speed, 4–5

Q

Quality of life, 6–7
enforcement of, 2–4

R

Racial profiling, 57, 60–68, 86
definition, explanation, and
justification for, 60–62
End Racial Profiling Act
of 2001, 130–131
history and evolution
of, 62–68
Rampart scandal (Los Angeles),
22, 31, 68–69, 73,
82–83, 97
Rational profiling (criminal
profiling), 61
Receipts for police-citizen contacts,
134–135
Recruiting and hiring
from the community, 127–128
people of good character,
128–130
Resisting arrest, 106
Respect, 145–147
Role models, 132

S

Safety of police officers, 44–52, 102
equipment and training
and, 47–49
turning on the "radar" and,
45–47
Safir, Howard, 69, 70
Self-arrest, citizen's, 135
September 11, 2001 events, 74–75
"Seven veils," 35–38
Silence, code of, 30–31, 41–42,
84–87
St. Petersburg Times, 87
Stopping citizens
on the street, 57
in a vehicle, 55–58, 105–107